For all those seeking a relationship wit_____ to Manifest Your SoulMate with EFT, is _____ ing EFT are given in a clear and easy process _____. You will learn to move beyond the blocks that are keeping you from the love that you desire in a fun and easy way. Don't be surprised if the tools you learn to use will help you with much more than just attracting love!

— KAREN L. WILL, MA, LPC,

www.whenhorseswhisper.com

Annette Vaillancourt has created not just a manual on how to manifest your soulmate, but a deep work that will create transformation throughout your life. Her questions are profound. If you're ready for some solid transformation, this book can help.

— PAMELA BRUNER,

author of *Tapping into Ultimate Success*, Business Coach, EFT Expert,

www.MakeYourSuccessReal.com

Annette has taken EFT to another level – using it to find a SoulMate. I have no doubts readers will find this book worthwhile and fulfilling, as they learn "tapping" to clear all those old life issues which burden them down and keep them from accomplishing what they want out of life.

— SHERRIE RICE SMITH, R.N. (Ret.), B.A., EFT-EXP,

Mentor of Christian Women, Certified Emotional Freedom Techniques Practitioner

www.eftforchristians.com

This book is upbeat, fast paced and inspirational. Dr. Vaillancourt offers a plan for bringing more love and happiness into your life using EFT tapping, a unique and powerful acupressure technique that is now being used throughout the world. The reader will learn to identify and clear any fears and underlying blocking beliefs that might push love away, and replace them with self-love and a positive life view. Her specific examples of how to use the EFT method make this a very useful book.

— GLORIA ARENSON, MFT, DCEP,

Author – Therapist – Teacher,

www.GloriaArenson.com

This amazingly powerful book speaks to the soul. Annette is relatable and really "gets it" on a level that is so reassuring and hopeful. She describes the tapping process better than any I've seen. The menus woven throughout the book are sheer genius, offering a customizable process that is sure to uncover and release any block holding you back. There's so much gold in this book, it goes way beyond manifesting your soulmate – it gives the reader the tools to manifest whatever it is they truly desire in their life!

— MARCI TRAYLOR, CPC, ELI-MP,
Professional Empowerment Coach, founder and creator
of the Shift To Clarity Coaching Program, www.marcitraylor.com

I wholeheartedly agree with the premise of How to Manifest Your SoulMate with EFT – the process of finding your life's partner is a spiritual journey and can absolutely be filled with joy and light. Annette Vaillancourt's book uses the power of EFT in a way I resoundingly endorse!

— ALINA FRANK, EFT Coach,
creator of www.whentoendit.com

The cutting-edge spirituality and compassion of Thich Nhat Hanh, and the postmodern physics of Deepak Chopra unite in sacred quantum harmony in the form of this groundbreaking work. Your SoulMate is always there and has always been there. Like the mighty Ganesh, Annette's EFT instructions will remove the deep-seated obstacles that occlude the spirit from manifesting your Vajra Consort, your transcendental partner on the path of Life, Interbeing, and Awakening. Annette has indeed channeled a body of awe-inspiring primordial wisdom from a higher, divine source.

— LAITH NAAYEM, Licensed Acupuncturist,
Former Buddhist Monk
www.LANacupuncture.com

Annette is wise, insightful AND practical – a rare combination! She invites the reader to explore his/her own soul as a necessary step to finding a mate, and she provides simple but profound exercises to guide that exploration.

— PAM HUGHES, M.Ed., LPC,
Teacher and Counselor

Annette Vaillancourt has tackled a subject near and dear to many of our hearts. How to Manifest Your SoulMate with EFT is written in clear language with steps that are easy to follow and examples that illustrate how you can change your life. Annette has a unique way of explaining and using Emotional Freedom Technique to remove your blocks and begin to enjoy life with your soulmate.

— LUCY MOORMAN,
Writer, Photographer, Energy Therapist

Even though I have done EFT on my own, it was very helpful to work with Annette and learn how to create my own unique tapping phrases. Knowing what to say when tapping was one of the things that tripped me up when tapping on my own. Now I feel much more comfortable creating my own phrases.

— ANGIE BUCKNER

Although I live with my SoulMate (yay!), I think this book is an affirmation of our relationship and will provide ideas for deepening it. Of course, being our own SoulMate is so important. This book will help illuminate that loving process for each of us as individuals.

— MEG BERRY,
Owner, Spa for the Soul

Thought provoking, heart provoking, soul provoking...EFT and soul work for smarties...a practical, fun, insightful way to continue your spiritual journey and manifest your heart's desires.

— LINDA COOK,
Teacher

What a wonderful compilation of information and tools written in a way that inspires the reader to create and manifest all that their heart desires. EFT is a very powerful tool beautifully described and made very accessible to readers by Annette...A beautifully written heartfelt book.

— AILEEN NOBLES,
Intuitive EFT Practitioner~Author~Hypnotherapy, Malibu Healing Center,
www.aileennobles.com

ANNETTE VAILLANCOURT, PH.D.

HOW TO *Manifest* YOUR SOULMATE WITH EFT

Relationship as a Spiritual Path

Love Your Life

How to Manifest Your SoulMate with EFT
Copyright © 2014 by Annette Vaillancourt.
All rights reserved.

For more information about this book or the author, visit:
www.ManifestYourSoulmateWithEFT.com

Love Your Life Publishing
A Division of Caelestis, Inc.
427 North Tatnall Rd. #90946
Wilmington, DE 19801
636-922-2634

ISBN: 978-1-934509-73-9
Library of Congress Control Number: 2013957028
Printed in the United States of America
First Printing 2014
Cover and internal design: www.Cyanotype.ca
Editing by Lynne Klippel and Gwen Hoffnagle
Chapter 4 illustration used with permission of Laurence Brockway
Author photograph by Menagerie Models

Disclaimer: This book is designed to provide information and education to readers. It is sold with the understanding that the author is not engaged to render any type of psychological, legal, or any other kind of professional advice. No warranties or guarantees are expressed or implied. Neither the publisher nor the author shall be liable for any physical, psychological, emotional, financial, or commercial damages, including, but not limited to, special, incidental, consequential or other damages.

This book is not intended as a substitute for the treatment of mental health issues or as a form of couples's counseling. The reader should regularly consult a licensed mental health practitioner in matters relating to his/her psychological and emotional health, particularly with respect situations involving chronic mental illness, substance abuse, trauma, suicidality, domestic violence or other severe psychological issues which that may require diagnosis or medical attention.

Disclosure: The characters in the book are not real persons. Any resemblance to anyone living or deceased is purely coincidental.

DEDICATION

To My Beloved:

May I be filled with lovingkindness.
May I be safe from inner and outer dangers.
May I be well in body and mind.
May I be at ease and happy.

May you be filled with lovingkindness.
May you be safe from inner and outer dangers.
May you be well in body and mind.
May you be at ease and happy.

May all Beings be filled with lovingkindness.
May all Beings be safe from inner and outer dangers.
May all Beings be well in body and mind.
May all Beings be at ease and happy.

 BUDDHIST PRAYER FOR LOVINGKINDNESS

TABLE OF CONTENTS

INTRODUCTION

HELLO BELOVEDS!

What if you could open up fully to love, live your purpose and share your gifts completely in and through a partnership with your SoulMate? Wouldn't a little struggle for clarity be worth it? Wouldn't some temporary (I promise!) discomfort be worth it in order to manifest the love of your life?

I hope so! I hope this is why you were drawn to this book.

Aren't you tired of "trying to find" love? What if you could clear all your internal barriers and just BE love? Of course, you'd become incredibly alluring, especially to your SoulMate.

When you live as a fountain of abundant love, instead of an empty well waiting to be filled by a lover, you will attract your SoulMate. When you have clarity and commit to manifesting your heart's desire, you will be drawn to those who light you up on every level... and they will be drawn to you. You won't waste time looking for a needle in a haystack. The needle will find you. When you quickly and effortlessly (well, almost) identify and permanently remove your fears, doubts, past hurts and attachments to old loves, a transformation takes place. You become the person your SoulMate finds irresistibly scrumptious. When you allow for love, become truly self-nurturing and then surrender to the perfection of divine timing, all anxiety and despair (so unattractive anyway) melt away. You live a life of fulfillment, equanimity, gratitude and purpose. That is what puts you on a trajectory – in fact, a collision course – with your SoulMate.

This book gives you simple tools and techniques to easily and quickly uncover and remove all the internal barriers that stand between you and your SoulMate. I feel so happy for you because I know without a doubt that this works. I know from experience that you can and will manifest any dream your heart desires.

I am excited about the transformational journey ahead. I am awed at the beautiful synergy the two of you will create. I am grateful for the powerful love you will share with each other and the gifts that your collaboration will bring to the world. Thank you in advance!

I want to share with you why I've decided to become the Elite SoulMate Coach. I've heard that if you have a big enough "Why?" you will stay motivated. I'm going to try to put it into words as best I can, though I hardly feel adequate to the task. **I feel called to do this.** This work blends together so many of my values and talents.

What I intend to manifest for and with my clients is a SoulMate, not just someone to date, but someone your soul needs to evolve. Let me be clear. I am not a matchmaker or a dating service. I am a *Soul*Mate coach and a facilitator.

I have always been keenly interested in spirituality, and this is the most spiritual work I can think of... helping people to be more loving and to evolve spiritually in and through their most intimate relationship. That alone makes my toes curl with delight!

This vocation calls upon me to continue to evolve and become more loving and open-hearted, and to practice what I teach. Integrity is a strong value of mine. It also calls upon me to be transparent, therefore vulnerable, and not hold myself up as knowing the outcome. I am just a facilitator of what I think of as a spiritual process that asks people to trust in a higher power – that of Love.

When I was growing up we sang a song in church called "God is Love." It took a while for the reality of this message to sink in. Now I believe this and do my best to live this. Love is how God manifests in the world. I always pray to do God's will. I believe this is what He is asking of me now.

More important, I am entering the "leave a legacy" time of life. I can think of nothing more satisfying than helping other people manifest their SoulMates too! When, not "if," that happens, I know I will die happy.

"The minute I heard my first love story,
I started looking for you, not knowing
how blind that was.
Lovers don't finally meet somewhere.
They're in each other all along."

RUMI

Chapter 1

HOORAY!
YOU'RE STILL SINGLE!

"When will I meet him?"
"We meet our soulmates when we're on our soul path."

 Karen M. Black

I KNOW YOU. I know you because I was you and I have coached and counseled you. You want success in love, but you're blocked, disappointed and frustrated. You are a good catch but still can't manifest the deep, SoulMate connection you desire. You are discouraged. Maybe you believe that all the good ones are taken. You obsess over the one that got away, or the one you want but who doesn't want you. You get a lot of first dates, but few second and third dates. You harbor secret fears and insecurities. You wonder, "What's wrong with me?"

What about what's *right* with you, even though you are still single? If you want to manifest your SoulMate, shift your energy and your underlying beliefs about what is possible. That is what this book will help you do.

So I say, congratulations! When everyone else is distressed and wondering:

- Why is love so elusive?

- Where is my SoulMate?

- Is there somebody out there for me?

- Why haven't I found my SoulMate yet?"

…you are seeking the ultimate relationship experience. You seek to manifest a SoulMate. That's what drew you, perhaps synchronistically, to this book.

Unlike your unhappy peers, you are looking for a deeper, more profound connection than you have ever had. You are looking for someone with whom you can be whole, healed and therefore holy, who challenges and supports your personal and spiritual evolution, partners with you in the mutual fulfillment of a higher purpose and channels Divine love into your life.

This is not to say that you are without frustration. You might even be puzzled and impatient. But you are committed to having your heart's desire and that's the most important issue.

The "Spirit" of the Times: The SoulMate Quest

During my 24+ years as a psychotherapist and marriage/couples counselor, and now as the Elite SoulMate Coach, I have witnessed firsthand the longing and struggle of today's singles and newly single people to find someone to love or with whom to share their lives. Most are genuinely confused as to why this hasn't happened yet or why their past relationships didn't work out.

Instead of attracting their SoulMates, they attract "losers," "users," "jerks" and "crazies." "Where are all the nice, decent guys?" "Why do the pretty women seem to go for the bad boys?" I hear their frustration. I empathize with their discouragement and fears of being alone and unfulfilled the rest of their lives. They are emotionally exhausted and frustrated by the dating game and trying to comply with "the rules."

Indeed, the spirit of the times is changing, and the changes of the times are towards the spiritual. A front page story in the April 2010 *USA Today* attested to this change. Research claimed that "72 percent of Generation Y agree they are 'more spiritual than religious.'" We are awakening and exploring other realities, including the final frontier of "inner space."

What we want in and from our intimate relationships is changing to match this spiritual groundswell. What we wanted and needed in our youth is not what we want and need at midlife or later. As we mature and evolve individually and as a culture, the goal of finding and nurturing romantic love is giving way to the goal of finding a SoulMate for the purpose of spiritual or evolutionary partnership.

Spiritual singles are now looking more for fulfillment and a deeper connection than that of the relationships of their youth or those of earlier generations. Kathryn Woodard Thomas, author of *Calling in the One*, says, "Relationships have changed more in the past 50 years than they did in the 5,000 years before." This is significant in that it suggests the speed at which consciousness is evolving and seeking new forms.

Once an esoteric topic, the concept of a *SoulMate* has exploded in self-help literature. Since 1990 a variety of best-selling books and tele-seminars have attracted national and worldwide attention on this topic, including:

- *The Seat of the Soul* by Gary Zukav (1990)

- *Journey of the Heart: Intimate Relationship and the Path of Love* by John Welwood (1990)

- *Soulmates: Honoring the Mystery of Love and Relationships* by Thomas Moore (1994)

- *Soulful Sex: Opening Your Heart, Body & Spirit to Lifelong Passion* by Dr. Victoria Lee (1996)

- *The SoulMate Secret: Manifest the Love of Your Life with the Law of Attraction* by Arielle Ford (2011)

People are waking up to an inner, spiritual longing for deeper, more meaningful connections that go beyond the economic, emotional and procreative motivations that prompted mating and marriage in earlier times. In short, the desire of today's singles is not simply for someone to marry, to take care of them financially or emotionally or with whom to raise children; today's singles desire a more spiritually fulfilling relationship – a SoulMate, not a cellmate, ego-mate or playmate.

Whereas traditional relationships are based on the hope of happiness, security and perpetual romance, SoulMates are the pioneers of human evolution. The "rules" no longer apply. Our journey is the hero's journey or the heroine's journey – the grail quest for healing. In the past, people seeking a spiritual path would retreat to a monastery where they could explore the deeper mysteries of life and cleanse their minds of all but what was essential. Today the SoulMate quest is an alternative to the monastery. It is a spiritual path for those who choose to remain engaged in the world. John Welwood, author of *Journey of the Heart: Intimate Relationship and the Path of Love*, says, "If enough of us can rise to the current challenges of the man/woman relationship, using them as opportunities to peel away illusions, tap our deepest powers, and expand our sense of who we are, we can begin to develop the wisdom our age is lacking."

As I was writing *How to Manifest Your SoulMate with EFT*, a wonderful synchronistic event occurred. I was contacted by three men in their twenties who wanted to film a documentary on dating. They wanted to explore the relationship between spirituality and dating! Thanks for the validation of my point here!

What Is a SoulMate?

"A soul mate is someone to whom we feel profoundly connected, as though the communication and communing that take place between us were not the product of intentional efforts, but rather a divine grace. This kind of relationship is so important to the soul that many have said there is nothing more precious in life."

Thomas Moore

For the purposes of *How to Manifest Your SoulMate with EFT*, I define a SoulMate as a spiritual/evolutionary partner:

- with whom you can be whole, healed and therefore holy

- who challenges and supports your personal growth and spiritual evolution

- who partners with you in the mutual fulfillment of a higher purpose

- who channels divine love into your life

A SoulMate relationship is a heroic journey, not without peril. As such, it is a catalyst for both personal and societal transformation. The focus of a SoulMate relationship is healing your *selves* and the world through conscious evolution and the expansion of your capacities to love and serve each other and all of humanity. At its zenith, the level of love, intimacy and commitment is high.

When I was growing up in the Catholic Church, we sang the song

"God is Love" with words from John 4:16. Love is a spiritual reality that lifts us out of ourselves and allows us to recognize unity and lay claim to our inherently Divine nature. Love is the process by which the Divine intersects with humanity and acts in the world of ordinary reality. As a friend's five-year-old daughter, Kaitlin, wrote, "You know... 'God' is a nickname for 'Love.'"

A SoulMate relationship, then, is a channel by which Love/God is brought into and shared with the world. When two souls join, 1+1 = the one/unity, or you+your SoulMate create Love = God. I am glad to see that Ram Dass agrees with me. In an interview, when asked about the existence of SoulMates, he said, "It's only one. There's only one of us. So what you're really doing is constantly marrying yourself at the deepest level of God marrying God."

In the end, you do not *find* your SoulMate, you *become* your SoulMate. Then and only then are you free to bond with another at this deep level.

How to Manifest Your SoulMate

Manifesting is the process of turning an idea, thought, belief or fear into a reality. As David Spangler, author of *Everyday Miracles*, says, we are manifesting all the time, though we don't do so consciously. If we are manifesting all the time, doesn't that make it a meaningless concept? No. A good analogy is breathing. While alive, we are breathing all the time. But there are poor ways of breathing and better ways of breathing that lead to relaxation, altered states of consciousness and better health. This is true of manifesting also. Yes, we are always manifesting, but we can train ourselves to manifest for specific purposes or for specific results, such as manifesting a SoulMate.

Manifesting your SoulMate is a spiritual process requiring an inner transformation that leads to outer manifestation. It is a deep shift in identity and awareness from a state of fear and limiting beliefs to a state of love, conscious choices, inspired action and co-creation with the Divine. It is about living in alignment with your higher purpose or *essence*. In doing so, you shift from *doing* to a state of *being* – being the one your SoulMate will be irresistibly drawn to.

As with any spiritual path, manifesting your SoulMate requires the relinquishing of ego and the re-visioning of lifelong beliefs. I'm not talking about changing your values, religion or politics; I'm talking about:

- getting clear about and making a commitment to having what your heart desires

- changing the assumptions you have about dating, men, women, love, sex, marriage and commitment

- tossing out old beliefs about not being "good enough" or worthy

- confronting and releasing fears

- uncovering and replacing unconscious beliefs that don't serve you

- learning how to practice true self-love and surrender

- releasing past attachments with love

- answering the "call to adventure"

- becoming more vulnerable, open and receptive

- allowing Spirit to guide you

I'm not saying your SoulMate quest is easy. No heroic journey is. As Theodore Roosevelt said, "Nothing worth having comes without effort." However, with the techniques and guidance through the seven stages of manifestation explained in *How to Manifest Your SoulMate with EFT*, you now have a roadmap and the means to achieve this goal.

My Story

I never wanted to get married, much less have kids. I witnessed the exhaustion of my Catholic mom, who had nine kids and no life. After helping raise the six younger siblings, I wanted none of that.

As a girl I was a tomboy. Athletic and fast, I could do anything my five brothers and dozens of cousins could do. Puberty and its physical changes was hell for me. I went from being one of the boys to running like a girl. I was humiliated and angry that my body betrayed me. Boys went from being my friends and playmates to vultures – ogling and grabbing at my developing body. This was not a welcome initiation into womanhood.

I didn't date at all as a teen and young adult. As a good Catholic girl I thought I had a religious vocation. I knew I had to be a virgin. Secretly I wanted to be a priest, but would have to settle for being a nun. Celibacy was no big deal to me. In my early twenties I looked into it seriously, spending weekends and going on retreats to discern whether I had "the call."

At 25 I was raped by a trusted co-worker, though I didn't recognize it as acquaintance rape until graduate school. With what felt like a "sacred wound," I left the idea of a religious vocation behind. I figured no decent man (including Jesus) would have me. Therefore I set about preparing to be single all my life.

It took me more than a decade to pull myself together and get through college and graduate school. I paid for all of it myself, often working three jobs while going to college. I was exhausted. With barely time to sleep, there was little room for a social life. Not that I wanted one. The whole idea made me too anxious and fearful. I became asexual.

In 1997 I got a wake-up call. My 39-year-old sister was killed instantly in a car accident. Her sudden death made me wonder if it was time to revisit my singlehood. I had never really stopped to think about whether I wanted to be single; I just was. I was 43 years old. I decided to start dating before it was too late. I wanted a chance at love before I died.

Dating was a nightmare because I didn't know what I was doing. I was not making conscious choices. I acted out everything that was stored in my unconscious. The social programming, sexual trauma and lack of guidance left me vulnerable to being used and confused. This confirmed the beliefs I had about myself, men and relationships. I was damaged goods.

It was so discouraging, but I kept going back for more. I thought I was just meeting the wrong kind of men. I had no idea what was really going on or what I was looking for. I blamed myself for not being the kind of woman men wanted. I went deeper into shame because I wasn't having a wonderful, fun time. Certainly something *was* wrong with me!

After breakups, I'd realize with horror that I didn't even *like* most of the men I'd had sex with. I'd be sexual too soon because that's what I thought I was supposed to do. I thought sex would get me the love I wanted. I was too nice or scared to say no. I realize now that after what had happened to me in my twenties, I just wanted to be normal.

Then came the epiphany. One evening later in 1997, I was listening to an internet radio show called "How Good Can You Stand It?" by Alan Hunkin. He was interviewing the singer Kenny Loggins. Loggins and his wife, Julia, had just written a book called *The Unimaginable Life: Lessons Learned on the Path of Love*. I remember exactly where I was – in the second bedroom upstairs. It had dark, stained, knotty pine paneling. A much-worn, harvest-gold, sculpted carpet that must have been there since the 1960s covered the floor.

I was mesmerized by the conversation because Kenny Loggins was describing a "conscious relationship… relationship as a spiritual path." He was talking about using a relationship to heal the wounds of the past, and not to keep reenacting them as I was. My mind exploded with recognition and my heart filled with hope. Suddenly my *still, small voice* was shouting at me, "That's what you want!"

Despite the epiphany, the journey was not over. I decided to stop dating until I could figure out why I was attracting the same kind of relationships over and over. Actually, that's not totally true. I decided to stop having sex until I was in love with someone and they were in love with me. Despite this conscious decision, I found myself falling into old patterns. I felt out of control.

Why couldn't I stop myself from making the same mistakes over and over? Why didn't I have the power of my convictions? Only when I mysteriously fell in love with a man who didn't have any romantic interest in me did I start to recognize that something outside of my awareness was at work in choosing my dating partners. That something was my unconscious and the unexamined fears that I had accumulated over my lifetime.

I didn't start seriously looking to manifest my SoulMate until my mother passed away in 2010. I felt that I had some obligation to stay single just in case my mother needed me to take care of her in her old age. This wasn't a conscious decision; that's what single daughters do. Looking back on it now I realize that powerful unconscious beliefs were running and ruining my love life. In short, I had continuously blocked my SoulMate from manifesting due to:

- **Barriers**

- **Beliefs**

- **Blindspots**

- **Biography**

- **Blahs**

It simply never occurred to me until my mother died that I might apply tools and techniques I'd gathered, tested and used so successfully over the years to the goal of manifesting my SoulMate. Six months later I developed and taught my first eight-week SoulMate ManiFest series. Before the class was even over, I'd met someone.

I'd love to tell you that he was my SoulMate because then you'd think I was truly a miracle worker. But he wasn't. Not even close. What he turned out to be was a powerful reminder that because I hadn't completed my inner and outer work – the same work I was teaching my students – I had gotten exactly what my unconscious was programmed to receive. I had manifested yet another fixer-upper. Today I am SoulMated, but – hooray! – I'm still single.

In all other areas of my life I had manifested amazing, even miraculous things, such as:

- **$70,000 in unexpected money**

- **A 70-pound weight loss**

- **My Brown Belt in Shotokan karate**

- **A permanent cure for my plantar fasciitis**

- **The sale of a second house (by myself) to the first buyer who walked in the door**

- **Doubling my income during the recent recession**

This path led to the book that is in your hands right now. I wish someone had told me or taught me what I am going to teach you. This is the book I needed when I had decided to start dating, especially once I knew that what I wanted was a SoulMate relationship. It would have saved me from so much emotional pain, wasted time and harsh lessons. It would have allowed me to consciously create the kind of relationship I desired.

The Work

To help you accomplish this transformation and guide you along the path of manifesting your SoulMate, each chapter includes both *inner work* and *outer work* designed to facilitate the next stage of the journey. The following exercises will prepare you to begin the process of manifesting your SoulMate through a guided meditation and a writing exercise.

Inner Work: You Just Call Out My Name

One of the first steps in attracting your SoulMate into your life is to live in *a state of feeling* that they are already in your life. The guided meditation below is designed to generate that feeling and signal your SoulMate to come to you. Try this meditation first thing in the morning and just before you go to sleep.

Find a quiet, comfortable place where you can sit or lie down. Do NOT try this while driving a car or operating machinery. You might want to record this meditation in your own voice or download it online from manifestyoursoulmatewitheft.com/readerbonus.

"Close your eyes. Let's begin by taking a few slow, deep breaths. Allow your body to release any tension… pain… or restlessness it is experiencing. Allow your mind to release any thoughts… concerns… or worries… just be in the present moment… aware of your breathing… slowly and deeply…. Allow your emotions to calm down… like a sea after a storm has passed… gentle waves of emotion that you notice from a distance… that lull you more and more and more deeply into a relaxed state… of complete presence in the moment.

"As you continue to relax... breathing slowly and deeply... start to notice a sense that you are not alone. This presence feels familiar, safe and comfortable... and radiates love and welcome to you.

"Allow yourself to imagine this presence is your SoulMate. Allow yourself to breathe in all the feelings of this presence... and the immediate connection... and recognition.... Notice your thoughts... emotions... physical sensations.... Really bask in all of those thoughts, feelings and sensations for a few moments.... Let them sink into your body and soak into your soul.

"As this sense of being with your SoulMate permeates your entire being... study it... memorize it... fix every aspect of it in your mind and heart.... You recognize this person... and it feels right in so many hoped-for ways.

"Bring your attention to your heart area.... Notice how your heart opens in the presence of your SoulMate.... Notice the qualities... the subtleties of those feelings. Savor the strong feelings... savor the subtle feelings....

"As you are basking in this experience, allow yourself to increase the intensity of this experience. Double the intensity of the feelings... then double that again... expand your heart's feelings until they take your breath away.

"As you continue to allow all of this experience... this bundle of concentrated thoughts, feelings and sensations... to expand... let it radiate outwards in any and all directions at once. Imagine you are sending a beacon of love... like a tractor beam... to your SoulMate. Release that beacon and send it as far into space and time as you need to... knowing that just by your intention and the positive, loving energy that you are sending that you are now in deep, deep connection with your SoulMate.

"Continue sending this signal for as long as you wish.... When you are ready, gently bring your attention back to the present moment, this room, this day and this hour. Take another deep breath, stretch your body and smile."

The next exercise encourages you to begin relating to your SoulMate today.

Outer Work: Wishin' and Hopin' and Thinkin' and Prayin'

"Imagination is everything. It is the preview of life's coming attractions."

ALBERT EINSTEIN

Why wait? Start your SoulMate relationship today!

You are already connected to your SoulMate by virtue of your desire to meet. Manifesting your SoulMate is inevitable. Your SoulMate relationship is a journey that takes place in the field of time and starts in the imagination. Since love is eternal – without beginning or end – why not start now instead of waiting for the physical manifestation of your SoulMate to occur?

Relationships are built on frequent contact, familiarity and openly sharing your thoughts, feelings, goals and dreams. Trust develops over time. Meaning develops as you discover who and how you are as a couple. Love grows as you take delight in sharing and being with each other.

One way to think about a relationship is as a conversation. Therefore a SoulMate relationship starts as a conversation on the soul level. Starting right now, you can share, listen to and exchange meaningful moments with your SoulMate within your imagination.

By starting a conversation with your beloved today, you put yourself in alignment with your SoulMate and speed the process of their physical manifestation. Instead of feeling the frustration, despair or sadness of not being in a SoulMate relationship, by engaging and exploring *now* you can shift your experience to that of excitement, eagerness and fulfillment. This makes you magnetic. Instead of waiting to *find* your SoulMate, start *relating* to your SoulMate as if they are already in your life.

Perhaps it would help to imagine that your SoulMate is away on a trip or lives at a distance. This is true if you think of the future as the distance between you. Then you are simply exchanging letters or emails or chatting until you are united or reunited.

For this and all subsequent exercises, I suggest you buy a journal to record your conversations and dialogues and track your progress. When journaling to manifest your SoulMate, choose a special notebook that has a nice cover that symbolizes that something special and sacred is contained within. You will want to keep your journal private. It is only for your eyes (unless you choose to share it with others).

When I first started this kind of correspondence, my letters to my beloved were mostly ones calling out for him to come to me. They were love letters. Pretty soon he started to respond to them! I know now from his responses why I love him so much! He is exactly who I dreamt he'd be.

As I went deeper into the process I struggled with the idea that I was just making it up. That struggle revealed a blocking belief. I didn't believe that someone like this existed! It's hard to manifest your SoulMate when you don't believe they exist. Wouldn't you agree?

Engage the Power of Imagination: Write Now!

Start a correspondence with your SoulMate. You can do this by writing letters to your SoulMate and then responding to letters from your SoulMate. Or you can write a series of dialogues with your SoulMate as if you are chatting online or face to face.

The magic is in sharing your heart's desire, then listening for a response and writing that down. Since the goal is a SoulMate who is the fulfillment of all that your heart desires, allow yourself to write a response that thrills you, challenges you to be your best and opens your heart even more to them.

Ways to Get Started

1. Call out to your SoulMate in a letter. Ask them to come to you. Tell them how you will recognize each other.

2.   Write love letters to each other.

3.   Share your thoughts, feelings and dreams on a regular basis. Only you will know how often is often enough.

4.   Reveal your longings and heart's desire to them.

5.   Tell them what turns you on and what you are passionate about.

6.   Ask them questions about themselves.

7.   Write letters of appreciation and gratitude.

8.   Buy or make them cards.

9.   Tell them your favorite ways to be romantic. Ask them what they like.

10. Ask them to help you find a solution to something you struggle with. Then return the favor.

What's Next?

In chapter 2 you will learn about the inner work ahead – the "final frontier" – that leads to manifesting anything you desire, including your SoulMate.

Chapter 2 ——————
The Royal Road to Manifesting Your SoulMate

"For one human being to love another; that is perhaps the most difficult of all our tasks, the ultimate, the last test and proof, the work for which all other work is but preparation."

Rainer Maria Rilke

THE SECRET TO manifesting your SoulMate is, as Rilke says above, in the preparation; in learning how to co-create with the Divine. What's "wrong" with you is that your ego fears and your self-limiting, unconscious beliefs are in charge.

Manifesting your SoulMate is a spiritual process. As Einstein said, "You cannot solve a problem from the same consciousness that created it. You must learn to see the world anew." Manifesting your SoulMate requires relinquishing the dominance of your ego and embracing the mystery and uncertainty of your soul's direction. The soul is the repository of wisdom and guidance, if only you know how to access it. It is the part of you that is already deeply connected to your SoulMate. It is the beacon. Ego is the barrier.

When you are not in touch with your soul, you cannot access the wisdom and guidance that arises naturally from it; there is too much chatter from fears and your ego clamoring for your attention. Thomas Moore says this of the soul: "It is a mysterious emergence that is seeded in eternity and is truly limitless. The power of this individuality is not forced but emanates from its own depths and inherent veracity." If you are not connected to your *soul*, how will you form a *Soul*Mate relationship?

To co-create with the Divine and manifest your SoulMate requires the ability to 1) shift out of your ego's fear-based thinking and into abundant, positive, connected thinking, 2) connect to and listen to the *still, small voice within* and 3) identify, change or replace unconscious limiting beliefs with consciously chosen desirable beliefs. In short, you need to get ego out of the way.

Writers in the literature of success and the Law of Attraction talk about the primacy of changing your beliefs and directing conscious attention to the object of your desires in order to manifest something you want. Your thoughts create your reality. If you are focused on "What is wrong with me?" instead of "What is right with me?" the answers will keep you stuck, depressed and defeated. When you focus on "What is right with me?" you get answers that hearten you and move you forward.

When it comes to manifesting your SoulMate, ignorance is *not* bliss. Self-awareness and willingness to move outside of your comfort zone are essential. Inner work uncovers the conscious and unconscious barriers, blocking beliefs, blind spots, biography and blahs so that you can eliminate them. Once you know what those are and remove them using the tools available in *How to Manifest Your SoulMate with EFT*, you are on the "royal road to manifesting your SoulMate." Yes, this process will take you outside of your comfort zone; but guess what? Your SoulMate doesn't live in your comfort zone.

Why would someone want a SoulMate relationship if it requires so much work? Well... why do people meditate? The benefits of a SoulMate relationship, as I've defined it, are the same as the benefits of meditation or any other spiritual practice. Meditation is not always pleasurable (especially if you are doing it right), yet there are multiple benefits to it, such as becoming free, awake, kind, compassionate and loving. In this context, when difficulties arise within and between you, SoulMates are mindful of them and see them as opportunities to gently dismantle any ego fears or self-limiting beliefs that stand in the way of your connection.

Barriers

Barriers are the fears that keep you from living and loving with your full potential. Fears keep you feeling separate. Unity is the spiritual reality. When you unblock *enough* – not all – of the fears that keep you separate from your SoulMate, your SoulMate will manifest in your life.

You might have barriers if you fear:

- **Nobody will love you**

- **Losing your freedom**

- **Conflict**

- **Being vulnerable**

Blocking Beliefs

These are the assumptions you hold at a conscious or unconscious level that limit how you view yourself and what is possible for you in the world of dating, love, sex, marriage and commitment. Most of my clients struggle with an inner conflict between what they consciously *know* or want to believe and the beliefs they *fear* are true. They feel it in their gut. More often than not, fear directs your behavior, even when you know better or want to behave as you would like to believe.

You might have blocking beliefs if you agree:

- There's no one out there for me.

- I am unlovable.

- All the good ones are taken.

- If people really knew me, they wouldn't like me.

- All others want is sex.

Blind Spots

Blind spots are traits and characteristics that you deny in yourself and project onto others. They are the *shadow aspects* of your psyche that you hate or idealize in others. These projected aspects, or blind spots, account for love or hate "at first sight." Because of unclaimed and unacknowledged blind spots, you do not see the world as it is; you see it as you are. You look at the world and other people's behavior through dirty glasses.

You might have blind spots if you think or say to yourself:

- I can't stand liars.

- I'll never be as talented/smart/pretty as you.

- People use other people to get what they want.

- She's too demanding.

- **He's nothing but a player.**

- **Skinny women are stuck up.**

Biography

Personal history and the roles you are assigned or assume in life significantly affect who you manifest into your life. Biography comes in the form of unexamined and unhealed life experiences, trauma, painful memories and continued attachment to old lovers. Releasing these attachments and old identities opens you up to new experiences and people.

You might be blocked by your biography if:

- **You secretly hope your ex will come back to you**

- **You were the one always getting dumped**

- **You identify with being the "irresponsible one" in your family**

- **You grew up in an abusive family or suffered any kind of trauma**

- **You are too attached to your parents or your own children**

Blahs

Living with passion and fulfillment draws your SoulMate into your life. In fact, it puts you on a collision course. Living a "blah" life draws boring people into your life. It puts you on a collision course with mediocrity.

You might have a blah life if:

- You don't know what you want to be "when you grow up"

- You feel aimless/depressed/worthless

- You don't know what your skills, interests, strengths and values are

- You only do just enough to get by

- You fear success or failure

Consequences of NOT Doing the Inner Work

"If you can't be a good example, then you'll just have to serve as a horrible warning."

CATHERINE AIRD

The consequences of not doing the inner work to remove the blocks and barriers are more than *not* manifesting your SoulMate. The habits that you do not break, the beliefs that persist and the fears that limit you will continue to bring the same kind of people into your life. As one woman in a recent workshop said, "I've been married to the same man four times – different names, faces and jobs, but essentially the same man."

There's something in depth psychology called a *repetition compulsion*. It's like being stuck in a loop that everybody can see except you. It is the tendency to keep repeating and/or creating the same kind of situations and relationships over and over in your life with the unconscious hope that you will find someone who will give you the love, security, happiness, etc. that you lacked as a child.

You might have heard the expression "Doing the same thing repeatedly, hoping for different results, is the definition of insanity." That's the essence of the repetition compulsion. Nowhere is this more painfully obvious than in dating. The danger is ending up in despair, frustration and pessimism. I've seen too many bitter, lonely singles give up on dating because they keep attracting the same kind of people over and over. If you have ever felt defeated or discouraged about dating, it could be because you believe that the same things will happen in the new relationship, and you unconsciously cause them to happen.

A second consequence of not doing your inner work is becoming or remaining a relationship (or romance) addict. If you are a relationship addict, you are in love with love. The temporary high of new love is what you seek. Unfortunately, no high lasts, so you crash when the infatuation stage wears off. You conclude that you were with the wrong person. You hurriedly find another one. You see relationships as disposable and interchangeable. Your goal is to feel good all the time by running away from the emptiness inside you.

Relationship addicts have a "hole in their soul." They try to fill the emptiness within with a rush of good feelings. Sadly they are always dissatisfied and are constantly on the lookout for "more" or "better."

What those seeking love are ultimately looking for is a connection with the Divine, with life and all that is – what author and philosopher Joseph Campbell calls "the ecstatic experience of being alive." Until you find that abundant source within yourself, you will manifest only ego-mates. SoulMates are soul-full people.

This is similar to the next consequence of not doing your inner work: dependency. According to couples therapists Gay and Kathlyn Hendricks, "You will tend to demand from others what you cannot give yourself. This demand places an unfair burden on those around you. It makes you a bottomless pit; no matter how much love they give, it is never enough." This is not SoulMate love.

It is immature to ask or expect romantic relationships to make up for the love and the nurturing you didn't get in early life. The time for that kind of love has passed you by. SoulMate love is not parental, co-dependent or one-way. You are not going to be pampered and taken care of as if you were a child. You might receive pampering and nurturing as an occasional gift, but you are expected to be able to function as an independent adult the rest of the time. You are expected to participate in a mutually fulfilling relationship in which give and take balance out over time.

We've all met desperate and needy people. If you continually find yourself in romantic relationships with those kinds of people, something in you is desperate and needy. This is your opportunity to remedy that.

SoulMate relationships support and encourage your maturation – emotionally and spiritually. Courage and inner work is required to discern and progress along that path. Yes, you might be impatient or tempted to make do with someone who is pleasant enough but who really doesn't help you grow and evolve. Why would you do that? The world is full of mediocre relationships. Why would you consciously choose to have one, or *another* one?

If you do not do the inner work necessary to manifest your SoulMate, don't be shocked if you are alone all your life. Time passes whether you are actively seeking to manifest a SoulMate or not. Why not improve the quality of your life, grow emotionally and spiritually, love and nurture yourself, and surrender to the mystery of life? A middle-aged woman at one of my presentations expressed a fear that this process would take too long. Since she is still single, I didn't quite know how to tell her that her way isn't working; I thought it was obvious.

If you ask people how many hours a week they put into manifesting their SoulMates, I'd bet the most frequent answer would be "None." People spend more time watching television than working to clear the barriers, blocks and beliefs that keep their SoulMates from manifesting. What are you waiting for?

The Benefits

"Creating space is often a question of clearing emotional debris. I cannot overstate the importance of doing this work as part of the spiritual journey."

JEFF BROWN

This is NOT a book that you read simply to gain information or a new way of looking at things. These tools and processes will *change your life* when you use them, just as they have and continue to change mine and those of my clients.

The first job I have as your SoulMate coach is to instill hope. Without hope that this process will bring you what your heart desires, you will see no point in going forward. I know that. Therefore I am not asking you to go on faith. I am asking you to make a commitment to use these tools, to complete every stage of this process and to learn for yourself. Be a skeptic like I was in the beginning… until EVERYTHING in my life changed when I applied these tools and processes.

When you embark upon the journey to manifest a SoulMate, you gain confidence by knowing that there *is* a SoulMate in your future. You feel, celebrate and live with the awareness that you are *already* deeply connected to your SoulMate; they just haven't manifested in the physical realm *yet*. By starting down this path, despair and frustration give way to hope. Hope gives way to certainty. Certainly gives way to excitement and positive anticipation.

When liberated from fears and self-limiting beliefs about what is possible, you successfully break the patterns that attracted the same kind of people into your life until now. New people and new *types* of people come into your life when emotional ties to the past are released. Because your *being* is different, your manifesting is different. In fact, you might be surprised by how magnetic you become!

Because you clear emotional baggage quickly and easily, you act and feel differently in each new relationship. Instead of carrying baggage over from one bad relationship to the next, you check it at the door. You become the person your SoulMate finds irresistible.

One of the greatest advantages of this process is increased courage and confidence. This allows you to open up, express yourself honestly, trust, take risks and try new things. Calm and confidence are two VERY attractive qualities.

Manifesting your SoulMate is about transforming your way of *being* instead of changing what you *do*. You become more self-accepting, self-nurturing, patient, clear, committed and willing to surrender to whatever comes your way. You live a happy, fulfilled life, expressing love from the abundant source within.

Inner Work: Memories… Like the Corners of My Mind

There is nothing as powerful as the stories we tell ourselves. We live out these stories and find people to cast in the various roles. In doing so, for every villain there is a victim; for every king, a queen. Reflecting on our past experiences is how we mine for the raw materials – the lead to transform into gold.

Your personal history of dating and romantic relationships is like a computer operating system that needs to be reprogrammed, especially if you haven't met your SoulMate. Listen to yourself tell stories of disappointment and heartbreak to friends or family. Notice that seldom do the details or the conclusions change. The stories seem frozen in time. They also tend to predict what you will manifest in the future.

The next two exercises demonstrate the power of stories. When you retell your past-love stories, you will discover themes and patterns. Then, in creating the SoulMate story you intend to manifest, you will begin to rewrite your inner programming.

I cannot stress too much the importance of taking the time to be thorough in completing these two exercises. You will learn what needs to be released, created or transformed. You will use the stories from these exercises in later chapters as well.

For the first exercise, to find out what beliefs and barriers you developed from past relationships and dating, recall all your past loves – from crayons to perfume. Go all the way back to your first childhood crushes. Write a short paragraph about each. Be sure to include what you learned, decided or concluded from each experience.

Below are three of mine. What I learned, decided or concluded from each experience is noted in italics.

"I had my first date at five years old. I got to go to Peter's house to play and drink grape soda. I remember blowing bubbles, which I do to this day when I'm feeling romantic. What I discovered was *I like boys.*"

I learned about the agony of longing when I was a teenager: "I had a spiritual connection to Danny in junior high school. Every day I saved the seat for him next to me on the school bus. I kept my eyes averted when he sat down. The only word we EVER exchanged was 'Hi.' On the days the bus was overcrowded, three people jammed into each seat. That meant that at times his body was pressed up against mine. I didn't dare breathe. I could hear my heart pounding in my chest. Surely he heard it also. *It was an agonizing awakening of longing and self-consciousness. I was the chubby girl who didn't wear makeup. I wasn't pretty and the boy I wanted hardly noticed me.* One time he made eye contact with me in catechism class! It felt like a jolt of unholy electricity. I remember that day like it was yesterday."

I learned about unrequited love and projecting my positive shadow aspects onto another person later in life: "When I met him, I was lonely and brokenhearted. Despite swearing off, I wandered back to the online personals for one more try. After our initial meeting, we saw each other every other weekend for several years. We weren't romantically involved, but I was in love for the first time in my life. Everybody thought we were a couple. The trouble was that I was deeply conflicted because I didn't see him as mate material, yet the feelings of unconditional love that flowed through me wouldn't go away. It was compelling and a joy to experience. In the end, this was my first real experience of unrequited love. *I was shocked to learn that loving someone doesn't guarantee they will love you back.*"

Reflection Questions:

- What themes or patterns are common among your stories? Longing? Unrequited love? Rejection? Hope? Pleasure? Fulfillment?

- What beliefs must you have held to attract those kinds of people and experiences into your life?

- What common traits or characteristics did your past loves have that either attracted or repelled you?

Outer Work: I Want a Man with a Slow Hand

For the next exercise, write your "SoulMate Love Story" that you want to tell your family and friends in years to come. This is your answer when someone asks you how you and your SoulMate met, grew in love and knew you were SoulMates. This is a powerful story, as it predicts your future. It is the harbinger of coming attractions. So write exactly what you want to manifest.

Write it with enthusiasm and in past tense, as if it's already happened. I love starting stories about what I intend to manifest with "Guess what!"

If it helps, you can fill in the blanks below to get started.

"Guess what! I met my SoulMate _____ weeks months ago. I didn't even know _____. When I first met him/her, I thought _____ and instantly felt _____. I didn't think _____. I was so happy when _____. The first thing that drew me to him/her was _____. I was so delighted to discover _____. Once we started talking, it was _____. I'd always hoped for somebody who _____, but I never expected I'd meet someone who also _____. I feel _____ and _____. How I first knew he/she was my SoulMate was _____ and _____. We've already discovered _____ about each other. As far as goals and life direction, we _____. I am _____ about that. I love that I get to share _____ with my SoulMate. The biggest challenge that we face together is _____. The vision that we share is _____. When we combine our energies, dreams and talents, _____. The gift that we hope to share with the community is _____. The way we challenge each other to grow and evolve is _____. When our egos get in the way, we _____. We recognize and receive Divine guidance in the following ways: _____, _____, and _____. What sustains our deep connection is _____."

As you write this story, note where your thoughts say, "Yeah, right! This will never happen." Write those down too, as you will use those doubts in later exercises.

Otherwise, celebrate this new story. You might want to read this story every day to reinforce it. Make it public. Share it with friends. You are predicting your future.

What's Next?

Chapter 3 addresses ways to manifest your SoulMate faster while following your bliss; emptying your cup; listening to the still, small voice within; and reveling in the synchronicities that follow. ✐

Chapter 3

MANIFEST YOUR SOULMATE FASTER

"As above, so below. As within, so without."

☞ HERMES TRISMEGISTUS

TRANSFORMING AND MANIFESTING are two of my favorite activities and the major themes of my life story. They also just happen to be what I love helping others do, too! That is why I call myself an alchemist, but you can call me your fairy godmother.

Clients often come to me feeling so discouraged or despairing that they ask, "Do you have a magic wand?"

"I do!" I respond, pointing to a place far from where we are sitting. "It's over there on the top of the bookshelf… gathering dust…" (I pause for effect), "because I have never had to use it."

I never have to use it because I teach a process for transforming your life so that by the time we are done working together you know exactly how you got where you wanted to go. You have learned a process. You have transformed *yourself.* Then, if life ever knocks you down again or you face an obstacle, you know what to do. Oh, and by the way, as you will learn in the next chapter, the magic wand is in your fingertips!

Much as I'd like to claim it as such, the process is not magic, even though it is mysterious. The surprise at the end of this process of transformation is that you will be able to manifest lots of different situations, material things and people (including your SoulMate) into your life.

Once you accept and embrace the transformation you will wonder why you were ever attracted to the kinds of dating partners that you used to be interested in. In fact, you'll wonder where they all went because you won't see them anymore. Remember, you see what you believe. You will attract different dating partners precisely because you are different.

YOUR FAIRY GODMOTHER SAYS, *"Wake Up!"*

"Manifesting a SoulMate happens because you believe it will. Believing is seeing. It will take as long as you think it will. It manifests when both of you are ready. Right now your SoulMate is preparing to meet you. When you meet, the timing will be perfect. Faster isn't always better. If they come to you before you are ready, you will not recognize each other.

"You are already connected to your SoulMate; you just haven't realized it yet. Start acting and feeling like they are already in your life – because they are already in your heart. Stop saying you are waiting, searching, looking or trying to find your SoulMate. These are all conditions of not having. Next time you are asked, try saying, 'I am in a SoulMate relationship. I just haven't met them yet.'

"Time is a human construct. It is an abstraction, not a reality. All that exists is the present moment. And all that exists is *in* the present moment, including your SoulMate relationship. That is why instead of longing for it, you should be celebrating it and living your life as if you are already with your SoulMate.

"When you are ready to stop running from your 'stuff,' your SoulMate will appear. What speeds up the process of manifesting is your willingness, ability and commitment to doing the inner work of transformation and releasing all that stands between you and your SoulMate.

"The goal is not to empty your life, put it on hold or sit around waiting for your SoulMate to appear. To speed up the process of manifesting your SoulMate, live a life worth sharing. Fill your life with activities, friends and interests that are expressions of your love and higher purpose. You become more attractive to your SoulMate when you are happy, so think and do joyful things. Live a soul-filled life."

First Empty Your Cup

"Your task is not to seek for love, but merely to seek and find all the barriers within yourself that you have built against it."

RUMI

In order to draw someone new into your life, first empty your cup of all that does not work – the barriers, blocking beliefs, blind spots, biography and blahs that block your SoulMate from manifesting. To empty your cup is to let go of what you think you know and rid yourself of attachments to past experiences and beliefs. You will use the tools and techniques described in chapter 4 to do so.

This is my adaptation of the old Zen tale, "Empty Your Cup":

A lovesick seeker went to visit a wise fairy godmother to ask for help in finding her SoulMate. While the fairy godmother quietly served tea, the lovesick seeker complained about dating, being too fearful, having to look good, the costs, the disappointments and her confusion about what men want. The wise fairy godmother just smiled and continued to pour the visitor's cup to the brim… and then kept pouring. The lovesick seeker watched the overflowing cup until she could no longer restrain herself. "It's overfull! No more will go in!" the lovesick seeker cried out. "You are like this cup," the wise fairy godmother replied. "How can I show you how to manifest your SoulMate unless you first empty your cup?"

Purpose: Now Follow Your Bliss

> *"The defining characteristic of soulmate relationships*
> *is shared purpose."*

CAROLYN G. MILLER

What does knowing your purpose have to do with manifesting your SoulMate? Living your purpose puts you on a collision course with your SoulMate. Your meeting is inevitable because you share paths that are in alignment and meant to converge at exactly the right time. SoulMates come together to fulfill a higher purpose and to create synergy in doing so.

Purpose is where your daily actions intersect with and reveal Spirit. Purpose is soulful action. Purpose is the hidden formula within your life – the summation and culmination of all your life experiences, gifts, talents, skills, values and dreams. Purpose is attained when you listen to and follow the still, small voice within. Purpose is revealed by your passions. Purpose is what makes your life make sense.

Whether you are aware of it or not, your life has purpose. There are many roads to discovering or revealing your life's purpose. Sometimes purpose is revealed to you upon deep reflection when you connect the dots across the span of your life. According to Gregg Levoy, author of *Callings: Finding and Following an Authentic Life*, sometimes purpose is revealed by a calling, a passion, a dream, a turn of events or the body simply wanting what it wants.

Purpose is the root of your life. Swiss depth psychologist C. G. Jung described life as a rhizome out of which everything manifests. It is whispered to you by the still, small voice from within. Sometimes the still, small voice seems like a strangled cry from the depths that is all too easily drowned out by the louder, more insistent voice of fear. Instead of living an authentic life that is authored from the soul, we often react to fears and live out old, unconscious behaviors and beliefs. Your purpose arises when you clear those barriers to living in full authenticity. It is that continuity that connects all of us to life and SoulMates to each other.

Why are you here on this earth at this time? What were you brought to life to do? Purpose connects you with your essence and your uniqueness, and motivates the utilization of your gifts.

What could be more soul-satisfying than to have your life's purpose be the thing that brings your SoulMate into your life? If you want to manifest your SoulMate faster, live your purpose NOW. I agree with Mark Twain: "The two most important days in your life are the day you were born and the day you find out why."

The following story, "Fatima the Spinner and the Tent," shows how destiny and purpose led her to find her SoulMate.

There was once a young girl named Fatima who was the daughter of a prosperous spinner. Her father taught her the ancient craft, and every day she would sit and spin fine threads of silk, dreaming of a man she may one day marry.

As she sat and spun she would sing, "Ah, life is good. Ah, fate is kind.

How happy I am in this life of mine."

One day her father said, "Come Fatima, I have business in the Middle Seas. Join me on this journey and perhaps you will find a young man worthy of your hand in marriage." So Fatima joyously sailed with her father, dreaming of the man she would marry.

A terrible storm, however, swept up, picked up the ship like a toy boat and crashed it onto some rocks. When Fatima awoke after the tragedy, she found herself washed up on the shore of some strange land. Her clothes were in tatters and the taste of salt was heavy on her lips. Worst of all, next to her was her father, dead.

Terrified, Fatima did not know what to do. But she heard a little voice inside that said, "Fatima, Fatima all is well. Why things happen, no one can tell." So she picked herself up off the shore and began walking. Soon she came to an elderly couple on the beach. Fatima told them of her lot and they told her that she was near Alexandria and that they were cloth makers.

"We have no child of our own. Please, come and live with us, if you wish!" they said. Fatima accepted their offer and learned the trade of her new life. She became a fine cloth maker and once again was happy. She would often sit and sing, dreaming of the man she would marry.

"Ah, life is good. Ah, fate is kind. How happy I am in this life of mine."

One day Fatima was walking along the beach where she had washed up so long ago. As fate would have it, slave traders were there. They snatched Fatima up, threw her onto a ship and sent her off to Istanbul. She protested bitterly, but to no avail, until one day she found herself looking out dejectedly among the stench of human flesh around her at the slave trade auction.

"How can this have happened to me?" she cried. There was no answer, except for the little voice within that said, "Fatima, Fatima all is well. Why things happen, no one can tell." It just so happened that it was a very slow day at the slave market and a wealthy mast maker saw the beautiful Fatima and took pity on her. He bought her, thinking that she would make a good house servant for his wife and that would better her lot.

But when the mast maker returned home, he discovered that a ship full of his cargo had been lost at sea. He had lost a fortune, and so he had to let go all of his workers. Then he, his wife and Fatima had to sit down and be the ones to carve the masts from trees.

In time, Fatima became a fine mast maker. Happy in her third life, she would often sing as she worked, dreaming of the man she would marry one day.

"Ah, life is good. Ah, fate is kind. How happy I am in this life of mine."

Fatima was such a fine worker that she became a trusted servant of the mast maker. "Fatima," he said to her one day, "I need you to sail to Java with this cargo of masts. Be sure to get a good price for them."

"I most certainly will," she cried proudly. Shortly she set off on her journey in charge of the cargo, dreaming of the good price she would get for her master.

But, as fate would have it, before she reached Java a terrible typhoon swept up and crashed her ship across some rocks. All was lost, and Fatima found herself once again washed up on a strange shore, her whole world lost.

When she awoke, this time she cried out with a fist to the sky. "Why is it that every time I think something's going to work out it only ends in frustration?" But there was no answer. Only a little voice inside said, "Fatima, Fatima all is well. Why things happen, no one can tell."

Fatima once again picked herself up off the shore and began walking. She met some people and discovered she was in China. Now, no one in China had ever heard of Fatima or her problems, but they had heard of a prophecy that a stranger, a woman, would arrive in China and that she would make a tent for the emperor. So when Fatima wandered into a town, people immediately, using sign language, said she must go straight to the emperor.

When she got there, the emperor asked her if she could make a tent.

"I think so," she said. "First I will need some strong rope." Strong rope? Nobody understood what she meant. So, Fatima, remembering her time with her father learning spinning, went out to the field, gathered some flax and spun it into strong rope.

"Now I will need some stout cloth," Fatima said. People rumbled among themselves, as they didn't understand those words.

"What is stout cloth?" they cried. So, Fatima, remembering her time among the cloth makers of Alexandria, spun some more flax into thread and wove it into stout cloth.

"Now I need some strong poles. About ten of them." Again, nobody knew what she was talking about, so Fatima herself went to the forest to cut down ten trees, and because of her time among the mast maker in Istanbul, she fashioned ten poles for the tent. Then she wracked her brain to remember where, in all of her journeys, she had seen tents. At last she settled on one and lo… a tent was prepared for the emperor. He was very pleased.

"Because you have fulfilled this prophecy, Fatima, you shall have anything you wish," the emperor said.

Fatima thought about what she wanted. "I will stay here. I wish to marry."

She married a fine prince and she had many children and many grandchildren. And as she lived her life and watched them play, she would often sing to herself, "Ah, life is good. Ah, fate is kind. How happy I am in this life of mine."

Listen to the Still, Small Voice Within

That still, small voice within is the voice of Spirit guiding you towards your destiny and helping you fulfill your higher purpose. It will also guide you to your SoulMate.

To hear your still, small voice requires time for quiet reflection. By allowing yourself time for getting quiet, you enter into the co-creative process with the Divine. When you are able to listen, the still, small voice speaks the truth. I advise you to follow it.

Try writing a dialogue with your still, small voice in a journal you set aside just for this SoulMate work. Ask that wise, compassionate part of you a question and simply wait for an answer to arise. Allow whatever comes to be your answer. Don't think or force anything. Just listen. Listen deeply.

How do you know you're not fooling yourself? The still, small voice is compelling and compassionate, and challenges you to be better than you are right now. How do you know you can trust its guidance? Try it and observe the results you get. More than likely it will ask you to go outside of your comfort zone. Hooray! That's exactly where you need to go. That's where your SoulMate is walking their path to meet you.

Synchronicities: Take Note of the God Winks™

When you are living your purpose and listening to the still, small voice within, you will notice an increase in synchronicities – what author SQuire Rushnell calls God Winks™. I take these synchronicities as signs and encouragement that I am being helped and that I am on the right track. When your conscious and unconscious are in alignment, synchronicities abound. Changes in beliefs, attitudes and behavior feel effortless. What seemed scary, difficult or impossible before seems matter-of-fact, easy or miraculous now.

One of my favorite God Winks™ was a time not too many years ago when I was suffering about something, possibly a breakup. I didn't know why things were happening to me, why things weren't going well. I was driving to my office lost in thought and praying for a sign to help me get beyond this negativity. Just as I was about to turn the corner at the intersection of the two main streets where my office is located, I looked up. On the SIGN in front of the church kitty-corner from me was the message "It's not about you!" I was so dumbfounded that I had to take a picture of the sign! I used that photo as the screensaver on my computer for a long time.

Follow the Yellow Brick Road: The Stages of Manifesting

Manifestation is not for the faint of heart but for the open-hearted and the full-hearted. This is a hero's/heroine's journey for the person committed to manifesting their SoulMate and being of service to humanity. There are predictable and necessary stages along the way, and a commitment to *surrender*. Chapters 5 through 12 are devoted to each stage of the journey.

The title of this chapter, "Manifest Your SoulMate Faster," is relative. Faster than what? Faster than you have done so far. Faster than you will go without these techniques and processes. When you set a goal like this, surrender is part of the process. It means that as you evolve and grow, you trust the Divine in the co-creation of your SoulMate relationship. There's no telling how fast Spirit will bring your SoulMate to you. What I am certain of is that you will not manifest your SoulMate doing what you have done so far.

Inner Work: I'm a Beginner!

As before, find a quiet, comfortable place where you can sit or lie down to do this exercise. Do NOT try this while driving a car or operating machinery. You might wish to record this exercise in your own voice or download it online at manifestyoursoulmatewitheft.com/readerbonus.

"Close your eyes. Let's begin by taking a few slow, deep breaths. Allow your body to release any tension… pain… or restlessness it is experiencing. Allow your mind to release any thoughts… concerns… or worries… just be in the present moment… aware of your breathing… slowly and deeply…. Allow your emotions to calm down… like a sea after a storm has passed… gentle waves of emotion that you notice from a distance… that lull you more and more and more deeply into a relaxed state… of complete presence in the moment.

"As you continue to relax and release, watch for a sensation of not knowing. This is the beginner's mind… the empty cup… open and curious… present… ready to respond… but without thinking ahead… no planning… just readiness…. How peaceful… even blissful this feels.

"If your mind should wander, try anchoring it to your breath. Simply follow the sensation of your breathing… in… and… out. Notice the cool air in your nostrils… the back of your throat… the sensation of your lungs filling up.

"Imagine yourself as a newborn baby… only minutes old… free of any pre-conceptions of what life is like… full of wonder… beginner's mind… an empty cup. Bask in this feeling… anchoring your mind, body and emotions there so that you can draw upon it… using the memory of this experience to guide you back to it at any time. Really bask here for a few moments…. Let whatever is present be with you in the moment and for this moment only… let this sink into your body and soak into your soul.

"Continue to connect with beginner's mind for as long as you wish…. When you are ready, gently bring your attention back to the present moment, this room, this day and this hour. Take another deep breath, stretch your body and smile."

Outer Work: Looking Forward to Looking Back

In alchemy, one of the chief aims was to turn base metals such as lead into gold. In our work, base metals are represented by your past beliefs, fears, doubts, past attachments and negative memories. To find the lead to turn into gold, go back to your "old" love stories that you wrote in chapter 2. Pull out the themes, limiting beliefs, fears and doubts that still resonate or have some emotional intensity for you in the present. Fill in the tables below.

In the first table write the list of self-limiting beliefs in the first column. In the second column, rate the intensity level of each self-limiting belief, with ten being the most intense discomfort you can imagine, and zero being absolutely no discomfort. (The first three lines are examples.)

Beliefs I Hold from Past Relationships

Self-Limiting Belief	Intensity Level
I am afraid there are no good SoulMates left.	10
I don't trust myself to pick the right people.	3
It stinks that there is no one out there for me.	8
•	
•	
•	
•	
•	
•	

Fears and Doubts

In the next table, list the fears and doubts that grew from past experience that you still carry into present dating situations. This is your emotional baggage. Rate the intensity level of that feeling on a scale from zero to 10 in the column to the right. (The first three lines are examples.)

Fears/Doubts from the Past	Intensity Level
I am afraid of getting hurt.	10
I doubt that I have what it takes to keep a SoulMate..	7
I am afraid no one will ever love me like my ex did.	9
•	
•	
•	
•	
•	
•	
•	

Past Attachments and Memories

Next list your past memories – hurts and attachments – that still have an emotional charge for you in the table below. As in the previous exercises, also rate the intensity level for each in the present moment. If there is a memory that has no emotional intensity left, it is already resolved for you. Only record the ones that still have an emotional charge to them. (The first three lines are examples.)

Past Hurts/Attachments	Intensity Level
I am deeply hurt that _____ said I was too selfish.	6
I am disappointed that things didn't work out with _____.	10
I am devastated that I lost _____.	20!
•	
•	
•	
•	

What's Next?

In chapter 4 you will learn the basics of the Emotional Freedom Technique and start using it right away. This puts the magic at your fingertips.

Chapter 4

EFT TAPPING: THE MAGIC AT YOUR FINGERTIPS

"Of all the creatures of earth, only human beings can change their patterns. Man alone is the architect of his destiny. …Human beings, by changing the inner attitudes of their minds, can change the outer aspects of their lives."

WILLIAM JAMES

What Is the Emotional Freedom Technique?

EMOTIONAL FREEDOM TECHNIQUE (EFT) was developed by Gary Craig, a Stanford-trained engineer who was passionately interested in personal development. He trained with Dr. Roger Callahan in Thought Field Therapy (TFT), a similar acupressure/tapping technique, but one requiring the user to remember numerous combinations of tapping points for specific issues and ailments. Gary's contribution to the field was to reduce the complexity of TFT to such an elegantly simple version that even beginners get amazing results.

In my experience, EFT is a quick, painless way to reduce or eliminate anxiety and stress by tapping on points about the face, body and hands. I have also used it to change strongly held negative beliefs by pairing it with affirming, positive thoughts. You stimulate acupressure points by gently tapping on them. While tapping, you simultaneously focus on a distressing thought, memory, fear or limiting belief in order to clear it.

How I Came to the Emotional Freedom Technique

Even though I'm smart, sometimes I'm slow to recognize a good thing. But when I do I definitely know how to capitalize on it.

I first learned about EFT in 2005 from a coaching colleague who offered a three-week teleseminar on "EFT to Overcome Food Cravings." After a brief introduction to EFT and how to tap, we were to have our food of choice with us for the first class. Since I was a lifelong chocoholic, I decided to test EFT using chocolate. I could never imagine giving up chocolate. My craving for chocolate was always at a ten on a ten-point scale. As I used to say, "Chocolate… it's not just for breakfast anymore!"

I wish I could say that I had what EFT founder Gary Craig calls a "one minute wonder" and never ate chocolate again. We tapped. I was skeptical. I felt hopeless in the grip of this addiction. I might have gotten my craving down from a ten to a three, but I didn't persist. In fact, I don't think I attended the next two classes. I told myself I was too busy and I'd listen to the recordings later. I never did. Truth is, I wanted a miracle and didn't get one. I was embarrassed.

I most certainly did NOT give up chocolate after one try at tapping. Like many others who have a long-term issue, I wasn't ready at the time to really use the technique. My addiction to chocolate ran much deeper than a simple craving. So I put the technique aside and chalked it up to "that's interesting, but not for me."

Months later, something triggered a panic attack. I hadn't had one for years. I'd gone to therapy. I was supposed to be over this. I think I'd just gotten dumped via email by someone I'd been dating for about 10 months. Even though the guy wasn't suitable for me at all – certainly NOT a SoulMate – it didn't matter. Suddenly I didn't feel safe. My mind was stuck in the loop of this thought and my body responded accordingly – racing heart and a creepy crawly feeling on my skin that was rising up my body to my throat. I just wanted to scream or jump out of my skin. I was on the verge of a full-blown panic attack. The intensity was at ten. It was bad!

Then I remembered the EFT tapping. I was desperate. I started tapping, *"Even though I think I'm not safe, I deeply love and accept myself."* One round. Two rounds. I was tapping fast and furious and crying at the same time. My mind went back to past traumas. Oh, my God! I didn't want to revisit that!

I kept tapping. *"Even though I wasn't safe then, I'm safe now."* One round. Two rounds. Three rounds. Better. Things were starting to calm down inside of me. I kept tapping. *"Even though I don't feel safe now, I've always been safe."* Hey! Where did that come from? *"I wouldn't be alive if I hadn't always been safe or found a way to be safe."* Holy Cow!

I felt much better. I kept tapping. *"Even though I assumed I wasn't safe, I've always been safe."* A smile, then a grin, spread across my face as I tapped. I kept tapping. Pretty soon I was so happy that I jumped up and started dancing and spinning around for joy! "I'm safe! I've always been safe! Whee!"

I looked at the clock. Five minutes had passed between the first sign of the panic attack to dancing around for joy. EFT had allowed me to erase the physical and emotional symptoms of the panic AND have a spontaneous cognitive shift also. That got my attention!

Why I ~~Like~~ LOVE EFT

It's about the results. I get better, faster, more amazing results for myself and my clients with EFT than from anything I'd learned about how to affect change during my Ph.D. studies in psychology. And it's not just change. It's transformation.

When I manifested an extra $70,000 in a year and doubled my income during the recent recession, using EFT, I didn't just change a few habits or market more. I transformed myself into someone who was abundant in all things. When I lost 70 pounds and earned a Brown Belt in Shotokan karate, I didn't just go on a diet and take a class. I transformed myself into a fit, lean person and a future Black Belt.

Personal transformation is a shift in identity. You don't just change what you *do*, you change who you *are*. Gautama *became* Buddha. Jesus *became* The Christ. Personal identity, as we commonly speak of it, is what we think of as "I." Personal transformation is what takes us outside of that limited "I"dentity and moves us into our purpose-full, higher, spiritual self. This is where true SoulMates connect. Otherwise it would just be ego-mates.

Incidentally, I used to refer to EFT as an "erasure for emotional pain." That was good enough for me at the time. Since then I've discovered that EFT produces "epiphanies on demand." For example, I often tap about something that I "don't know." In the course of tapping I often have an epiphany that reveals that a part of me did and does know the answer; I just had to get my anxiety and not-believing out of the way.

Such epiphanies are also the precursors of synchronicities – meaningful coincidences. One time I was tapping away a little distress over someone not responding to my emails and texts. Literally the second that I completed my tapping I received a text from him. That has happened a couple of times since then. Talk about speedy results! Once a barrier is removed, Spirit brings you just what you need at that moment you need it.

One of the key concepts in manifesting a SoulMate is to become the person that your SoulMate would be attracted to. That doesn't mean hit the gym and color your hair. In my view that means become your courageous, infinite self. That is what I am inviting you to do throughout this book. EFT is a wonderful tool that will aid you in that transformation.

How to Use EFT

A simplified overview of EFT is all that's necessary here. You do not have to "believe" in EFT for it to work. EFT is a cousin of acupuncture, which has a 5,000-year history. It falls under the rubric of *energy psychology* because it works directly with the subtle energy systems of the body. According to Traditional Chinese Medicine (TCM), illnesses are caused by a disruption of the flow of these subtle energies in the body. Health is restored by removing the energetic blockages, which allows the body to return to a natural state of health. EFT has revealed that *personal psychology* – that is, moods, thoughts and beliefs – is also affected by imbalances in the body's energy system. By removing those blockages, the intensity level of those upsets is rapidly reduced or removed altogether.

The Intensity Level

EFT works best when you focus on a very specific feeling, event, physical sensation, pain or memory that has a high level of emotional intensity *in the moment*. This is very important. Unless you experience intensity of feelings *in the moment*, there is no need to tap on an issue. *Before* you start tapping, you rate the intensity of the upset on a scale of zero to ten (low to high). This is your starting *intensity level*. You check again after you have done several rounds of tapping to see if something has changed. Intensity levels can go up or down as you tap. The goal is to reduce the intensity level to zero.

If the intensity level increases while you are tapping, it might mean that another *aspect* (explained below) of the issue is coming into awareness. You can choose to incorporate that into your current round of tapping or write it down in your journal to tap on later as a separate issue.

The Tapping Statement

In EFT the tapping is paired with a *tapping statement* that is designed to get your mind focused on and experiencing the intensity of the issue in the moment. Don't worry that it starts out with something negative. You will NOT be tapping this negative thought into your mind. *It is already there.* You use EFT to get rid of it. The tapping statement usually takes the form of:

"Even though I feel/think _____, I deeply love and accept myself."

A couple examples of tapping statements related to manifesting your SoulMate are:

"Even though I am afraid that there is no one out there for me, I deeply love and accept myself."

and

"Even though I am still in love with my ex and secretly hope they will come back to me, I deeply love and accept myself anyway."

Tapping Points

The *tapping points* are located around the face and torso of the body (see chart below). These correspond to meridian points in acupuncture. You do not have to be pinpoint accurate in tapping on these points, but you should be in the vicinity of them.

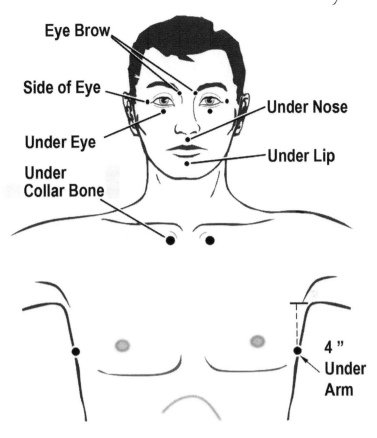

Graphic by Laurence Brockway

Getting Started Using EFT

To start using EFT, select a distressing emotion, issue, memory, or physical pain to work on.

- Create your tapping statement. Be very specific in describing the emotion, issue, memory, or physical pain.

- Determine your intensity level *at this moment.* While thinking of your emotion, issue, memory, or physical pain, rate how intense it is NOW. No sense working on something that has no intensity to it!

- Start tapping on the karate chop point, OR rub the tender spot while saying the tapping statement *aloud and with conviction* three times. It is important that you say it like you mean it!

Karate Chop Point

Graphic by Laurence Brockway

Tap on All Points

Next, starting at the top of the head, tap at least seven times on all the points shown in the chart above (except the tender spot) using your index and middle fingers together. Say aloud a shorthand version of the tapping statement, called the *tapping phrase*. For example, with this tapping statement: *"Even though I am afraid that there is no one out there for me, I deeply love and accept myself,"* a few basic tapping phrases would be:

Top of Head:	*"There's no one out there for me."*
Inner Eyebrow:	*"There's no one out there for me."*
Outside Eyebrow:	*"There's no one out there for me."*
Under Eye:	*"There's no one out there for me."*
Nose:	*"This fear I have..."*

Chin:	*"This fear I have…"*
Collarbone:	*"That there is no one out there for me."*
Underarm:	*"I am afraid there is no one out there for me."*

As you tap, watch for the impulse to sigh or yawn. Don't stifle it. It is a sign that your energy is shifting and most likely you are releasing your distress. Continue tapping gently on all points until you have reached an intensity level of zero. If your distress has dropped some, but not to zero, be persistent. Keep tapping additional rounds.

Working with Aspects

Some issues can be cleared quickly by tapping on a single tapping statement until your intensity level drops to zero. These are the "one minute wonders." However, most issues are more complex than that. Most goals have more than a single *aspect* blocking you from reaching them, so be vigilant for them and write them down when they arise.

Sometimes in the course of tapping on one issue, other feelings, memories or situations pop into your mind. These are new or related aspects. For example, if you are tapping to clear a fear of abandonment due to being dumped by a past love, your tapping statement might be: *"Even though I am terrified of being abandoned again, like when John broke up with me, I deeply love and accept myself."* While tapping, if you notice that your intensity level increases rather than decreases, this might signal the appearance of a new aspect. Perhaps you find yourself thinking about your parents' divorce when you were six years old. This memory is another aspect that is attached to the larger issue of abandonment.

When you are ready to work on the new aspect of a complex issue, create a new tapping statement for it. For the situation above, your tapping statement might be: *"Even though I was deeply hurt and felt abandoned after my parents' divorce when I was six years old, I deeply love and accept myself."*

Once you have that, determine the intensity level for the new tapping statement, then proceed to tap as usual.

Another way to work with new aspects is to incorporate them into the current tapping sequence. For example:

Top of Head:	*"I was hurt by my parents' divorce."*
Inner Eyebrow:	*"This hurt…"*
Outer Eyebrow:	*"I felt abandoned…"*
Under Eye:	*"Abandoned and hurt."*
Nose:	*"Hurt from my parents' divorce…"*
Chin:	*"Hurt and abandoned."*
Collarbone:	*"I never want to be close ever again…"*
Underarm:	*"And so I block closeness… abandon them before they abandon me."*

Complex issues like abandonment have multiple aspects. You do not have to tap on every aspect related to that issue to clear it from your life. You just have to tap on *enough* aspects to get the entire issue to "collapse." Then the effects generalize, meaning the *entire* issue goes away.

Growing Pains and Creating Safety

According to Gary Craig, most EFT beginners have an 80 percent success rate just learning EFT from his manual. EFT is one of the more benign techniques for personal growth that I have encountered. Still, it is a powerful technique, and you might encounter some growing pains and the need to make adjustments in your life – hopefully good ones – once you manifest your SoulMate!

That's not to say there are no risks. I want you to know what to watch for and what to do if you get into something you didn't expect. If you are working with a therapist for *any* reason, but especially if you have a history of sexual abuse or assault or have been the victim of domestic violence, childhood physical abuse or severe neglect, I strongly encourage you to let your therapist know when you start using EFT to manifest your SoulMate. EFT can open up unconscious material, both positive and negative, so use your therapist for support.

Because you will be starting out with issues that have a range of intensity levels, be aware that you are going to feel some discomfort initially in the process of tapping. The tapping itself is designed specifically for reducing and/or removing that intensity. As you become more proficient, you will learn how to create individualized tapping statements for your unique life situations. Sometimes issues increase in intensity before they reduce in intensity, so set aside ample time to work on an issue just in case there are multiple aspects associated with it. You might have to clear many aspects of complex issues, and this might not happen in one sitting.

To further ensure your emotional safety, be sure you know how to set this work aside so that you can resume daily life unhampered. To do so, you might want to open each EFT session with *"Even though I might experience some intense issues, I quickly clear them and enjoy my new emotional freedom."* To close an unfinished session in which there are more aspects that need work but you don't have time to do them right now, tap on *"Even though there's more work to do, I am calm, happy and safe."*

Another way to close an EFT session is to imagine locking all your remaining issues into a large, locked container: Close your eyes. Take a few deep breaths to relax. Call to mind a container of exactly the right size and strength in which you can safely store any unfinished work until the next time. Use all your senses to create this container in your mind. How big is the container? What color is it? What is it made out of? What does the opening look like? What kind of lock does it have? Where is it located? Is there anything surrounding or near the container? Are any words or pictures on the container? When you put your unfinished work inside and lock it up, what sound does it make when you lock it? When you sense that everything is locked up safely, open your eyes; take a deep, cleansing breath; smile; and re-enter your normal life.

If you find that while tapping you stumble across some repressed memories of abuse or start feeling suicidal, please contact a professional trained to work with trauma.

Inner Work: Think for Yourself

You might never have tapped before or even heard of tapping until now. And if you have done a little tapping for other things but need a refresher, this will be good practice for you.

You certainly might be a little skeptical about EFT. That's fine. I was too when I first learned it. That is, until I started getting amazing results! People who knew me before EFT knew that I was not a person who gushes about the latest fad or fashion. In my professional training, I was trained to be a bit of a skeptic. But, wow! As you read earlier, my life has totally changed since applying EFT to… almost everything. But don't take my word for it. You are going to learn how to do this for yourself and transform your love life.

Let's start by removing any skepticism you might have. Please refer to the tapping chart earlier in this chapter to refresh your memory as to the location of the tapping points. You will need paper and something to write with. Say this statement aloud and with conviction while noting any sense of hesitation, resistance, tightness in your body, catch in your throat or "yes, but" in your mind:

"I am skeptical that EFT will work for me."

Now rate the intensity level of that skepticism from zero to 10 with zero indicating no intensity and 10 indicating the highest intensity you can experience. Write that number down. Next create a tapping statement using this formula:

"Even though I _____, I deeply love and accept myself."

For this session we are going to start with:

"Even though I am skeptical that EFT will work for me, I deeply love and accept myself."

Begin, as you will each time, tapping at the karate chop point, repeating the entire tapping statement aloud and with conviction three times.

"Even though I am skeptical that EFT will work for me, I deeply love and accept myself."

"Even though I am skeptical that EFT will work for me, I deeply love and accept myself."

"Even though I am skeptical that EFT will work for me, I deeply love and accept myself."

Next tap at least seven times, using your index and middle fingers together, on each of the tapping points shown on the chart. Say aloud each of the tapping phrases below as you tap on each respective tapping point.

Top of Head:	*"I am skeptical."*
Inside Eyebrow:	*"This skepticism..."*
Outside Eyebrow:	*"I don't believe this will work."*
Under the Eye:	*"I don't believe this will work for me."*
Under the Nose:	*"I don't yet believe this will work for me."*
Chin:	*"I won't allow this to work for me."*
Collarbone:	*"This doesn't fit my worldview."*
Under the Arm:	*"This doesn't fit my worldview."*
Top of Head:	*"I don't believe this is going to work..."*

Inside Eyebrow:	*"But what if it does?"*
Outside Eyebrow:	*"What if it does?"*
Under the Eye:	*"How could it?"*
Under the Nose:	*"I don't understand it."*
Chin:	*"What if I don't have to understand it?"*
Collarbone:	*"What if I just allow it to work?"*
Under the Arm:	*"What if I just allow it to work?"*

Top of Head:	*"I don't understand how gravity works either…"*
Inside Eyebrow:	*"But I know it does…"*
Outside Eyebrow:	*"Because I can see the results."*
Under the Eye:	*"So why can't EFT be the same as gravity?"*
Under the Nose:	*"How about I just tap…"*
Chin:	*"And look for the results?"*
Collarbone:	*"The results are what are most important."*
Under the Arm:	*"Yeah, I want the results."*

If you notice yourself feeling an urge to sigh or yawn while tapping, allow yourself to do so. That is a sign that your energy blocks are releasing.

Top of Head:	*"Even though I may have a little skepticism…"*
Inside Eyebrow:	*"When I get the results I want…"*
Outside Eyebrow:	*"Does it matter if I understand it?"*
Under the Eye:	*"Maybe yes."*
Under the Nose:	*"Maybe no."*
Chin:	*"Maybe yes."*
Collarbone:	*"Maybe no."*
Under the Arm:	*"As long as I get the results, who cares?"*

Top of Head:	*"Bye-bye, skepticism."*
Inside Eyebrow:	*"Hello, results."*
Outside Eyebrow:	*"Bye-bye, skepticism."*

Under the Eye:	*"Hello, results."*
Under the Nose:	*"Thank you, EFT…"*
Chin:	*"For all the amazing results you are going to bring into my life."*
Collarbone:	*"Thank you, EFT…"*
Under the Arm:	*"For all the amazing results you are going to bring into my life."*

For the purpose of becoming proficient in doing this for yourself, it's your turn to create one round of reminder phrases like those we have been using above. Fill in the blanks and tap along to your own phrases related to feeling skeptical.

Top of Head: _____

Inside Eyebrow: _____

Outside Eyebrow: _____

Under the Eye: _____

Under the Nose: _____

Chin:_____

Collarbone: _____

Under the Arm: _____

Stop here and check in with yourself. Take a moment to go back and assess how intense the original statement feels right now.

"I am skeptical that EFT will work for me."

Write down the new rating next to the original rating and compare. If the rating is anything other than a zero, resume tapping using a modified tapping statement like this one:

> *"Even though I am still a little skeptical that EFT will work for me, I deeply love and accept myself."*

Go back to the karate chop point, tapping there while repeating this modified tapping statement aloud and with conviction three times:

> *"Even though I am still a little skeptical that EFT will work for me, I deeply love and accept myself."*

> *"Even though I am still a little skeptical that EFT will work for me, I deeply love and accept myself."*

> *"Even though I am still a little skeptical that EFT will work for me, I deeply love and accept myself."*

Top of Head:	*"I am still a little skeptical."*
Inside Eyebrow:	*"This remaining skepticism."*
Outside Eyebrow:	*"A little bit skeptical."*
Under the Eye:	*"I prefer results over skepticism."*
Under the Nose:	*"Yeah, I'll take the results."*
Chin:	*"If I have to do some tapping that I don't understand to get them…"*
Collarbone:	*"What do I care?"*
Under the Arm:	*"The results override a little bit of skepticism."*
Top of Head:	*"So what if I'm still a little bit skeptical?"*
Inside Eyebrow:	*"That's healthy."*
Outside Eyebrow:	*"That just means I'm discerning…"*

Under the Eye:	*"And I'm open to trying new things."*
Under the Nose:	*"I am open to trying new things."*
Chin:	*"I choose not to let a little bit of skepticism block me..."*
Collarbone:	*"From having what I want."*
Under the Arm:	*"Because I deserve to have what I want."*
Top of Head:	*"Good for me!"*
Inside Eyebrow:	*"Good for me that I am open to having what I want."*
Outside Eyebrow:	*"Good for me that I am open to new ways to get what I want."*
Under the Eye:	*"Good for me for knowing what I deserve."*
Under the Nose:	*"Good for me for giving this to myself."*
Chin:	*"Good for me for staying open."*
Collarbone:	*"Good for me for being a trailblazer."*
Under the Arm:	*"And so it is!"*

It is time to stop and check in again. Go back and assess how intense the original statement feels right now. Again, say aloud and with conviction:

"I am skeptical that EFT will work for me."

Rate the intensity level again. Write down that number next to the two others. Compare that to the last number you wrote down after the first round of tapping. Hopefully you gave it a zero. Hopefully there's a big grin on your face because you are now excited rather than skeptical about using EFT to manifest your SoulMate.

However, if your rating is still anything other than a zero, you just have to persist in tapping until you reach zero. If your intensity level went up, it is possible that another aspect has arisen that needs to be addressed.

Finally, if you are at zero, test to make sure there are no other aspects related to this shift: Close your eyes. Use your imagination to try to make the initial skepticism come back. Notice if there is anything else attached that needs to be cleared. If you feel the skepticism coming back, go back to the karate chop point and keep tapping on all the points, saying, *"This remaining skepticism…"* Sometimes you just need to persist in the tapping to clear something.

Congratulations! You have taken the first important step in manifesting your SoulMate!

Outer Work: A Change Would Do You Good

Go back to the "Looking Forward to Looking Back" exercise in chapter 3. Turn all those blocking beliefs, fears and past attachments into tapping statements. Write them in your SoulMate journal. For example, *"Even though I am afraid there are no good partners left, I deeply love and accept myself."* Or, *"Even though I am deeply hurt that my mother said I was too selfish for anyone to love me, I deeply love and accept myself."*

Next rate the intensity level for each of your tapping statements before you start tapping. Now you are ready to start. Keep track in your journal of which ones you have cleared. Oh, and please note what changes in your life as a result! Often after working with a client to clear something painful, they report, "Nothing has changed," when I see them next. Then they go on to report how everything has changed. They just hadn't realized it because the change now feels effortless.

An example of this, though it doesn't apply to SoulMates, is a client who came in terrified of making cold calls for his business. When I saw him about three weeks later, after tapping briefly to clear his fears of rejection, he said in a tone of surprise, "I LOVE cold calling." He hadn't even thought about his fear since that single round of tapping!

What's Next?

Chapters 5 through 12 introduce you to the stages of manifesting and how to apply EFT to any challenges you find in them.

Chapter 5

PAVING THE WAY: COMMITMENT AND CLARITY

"When we think about the specifics of what we would like to manifest in our lives, our visions should feel absolutely yummy: I mean an 'ooh-that-feels-so-wonderful' kind of feeling."

WILL DONNELLY

Making the Commitment

YOU ARE COMMITTED to being single. Gulp! There, I said it. If you are not in a SoulMate relationship, it is because some part of you has chosen to be single. You can protest all you want. If you want a blue Corvette, and don't have one, it's the same reason; you are resisting having what you say you want. Most likely you don't know why this is so… yet. In this chapter I will show you how to use EFT to remove fears and self-limiting beliefs about making a commitment to manifesting the exact SoulMate relationship your heart desires.

Making a commitment to your goal is the first step in manifesting. I said for years that I wanted to do something skillful with my body. It wasn't until I was 54 that I committed to doing something about it. I started karate lessons. I am currently a Brown Belt and have committed to becoming a Black Belt by 60. I made the commitment to having what I wanted. Until I made the commitment, nothing happened. Once I did, opportunities came to me in unexpected ways, including a free trip to karate camp.

That is why we are starting with making a commitment first. Without it, nothing will happen. To manifest your Soulmate, you need to consciously choose and commit to having *exactly* what you want. In other words, commitment and clarity go hand in hand. Without this, what you manifest comes out of your unconscious, confirming every fear about men/women, dating, commitment, sex and marriage that lies buried beneath the surface.

Most people think manifesting a SoulMate will just happen – that it's a matter of luck, knowing how to flirt or being in the right location. Not so. It's a matter of inner preparation. Think about it; if you wanted to advance in your career or get into the best shape of your life, would you think it would "just happen" or that it's a matter of luck, schmoozing or being in the right location? Just like all of life's other goals, manifesting your SoulMate requires commitment, clarity and action.

Inner preparation requires a specific kind of attention to inner cues. Perhaps you feel a sense of dissatisfaction, restlessness, frustration or yearning. That feeling might sound like "Is that all there is?" You become aware of a desire because of an epiphany, insight or the inspiration of someone who has met and committed to their SoulMate – if they can do it, so can you! Learning to listen to those inner cues, or the still, small voice within, is learning to listen to the voice of Spirit calling you to be something more.

There is magic and power in making a commitment to manifest your SoulMate. As Ralph Waldo Emerson said, "Once you make a decision, the universe conspires to make it happen." Once you make a commitment, gain clarity and clear blocking fears and self-limiting beliefs, amazing things start to happen. Synchronistic things start to happen that confirm that you are in alignment with what you desire.

Commitment is the frame that you put around the picture you've painted of your SoulMate. Commit to having all of what you need and some of what you want. Commit to a relationship with your SoulMate that starts immediately.

Your Fairy Godmother Says,

"Don't Waste My Time"

"Who you are committing to is your self. That is the scariest part. Any commitment you make is always between you and your self. The difficulty with that is we are creatures of excuses. The only person you let down or satisfy by your commitment is your self. Commitment opens the door for passion to emerge.

"If you can't commit 100 percent to having what you want, don't even bother trying to manifest anything new. It won't work. Yes, you deserve to have the best that love and life have to offer. The catch is that you have to commit to having it. Don't settle for less. Don't make me wave my magic wand over you for nothing!"

Getting Clear on What You Desire in a SoulMate

Manifesting a SoulMate is a collaborative effort with the Divine. Each is responsible for a different part. Your responsibility in the beginning is to open yourself up to receiving by making a commitment to having exactly what you want. Hone in and focus on the feeling you want to have and how you want to *be* in that relationship. Leave the details up to the Divine. Mike Dooley, author of the *Notes from the Universe* series, says that our job is to decide on the "what" and let the Universe take care of the "how."

Successful people know what they want. They live with certainty that what they want is coming into their lives. They are clear on the essence of what they want. They think about it, talk about it and, more important, *feel* about it. Your job in attracting your SoulMate is to be clear about what you are committed to and to commit to what you are clear about.

In any manifesting process, the secret is to focus on and experience in the present moment the *feeling* of what you want to draw into your life. This gives you the ultimate goal right now. Think about it; if you want love to come into your life, generate love, give love and act in loving ways right now – to everyone! You do not have to wait for someone special to come into your life to turn on your heart. This feeling of abundant love that is sourced from within is what makes you magnetic to your SoulMate. It is your "heartsong" that calls out to your SoulMate – drawing them into your life.

What do you truly desire in a SoulMate relationship? This is not the list of outer characteristics or personality traits that most of us have been advised to develop. I suspect many of you have such a list somewhere and are no nearer to manifesting a SoulMate than you were before you created your list. The reason this kind of list doesn't work is because it doesn't put you into energetic alignment or present-time relationship with what you desire. Most likely when you developed that list of characteristics and personality traits, you were focused on what you *didn't* have. You were in a feeling state of *wanting* instead of being in the feeling of *having received* what you desire. Since what you focus on increases, when you focus on the wanting, you live in a state of wanting. When you focus on having, you manifest faster. If you wait until you find a relationship to give love, to be soulful and to be the best YOU that you can be, you will waste your life. Live a fulfilling life – one worth sharing!

If you are going to make a list at all, make a list of the spiritual lessons you want to learn, the experiences you want to share, what you want to feel and the things you want to give to your SoulMate and the rest of humanity.

Write this list in present tense. For example:

- I am so grateful and happy that my SoulMate and I share a commitment to community service projects.

- I love giving my SoulMate foot massages.

- I love how I get to be completely myself when I am with my SoulMate.

- I love sharing my passion for music with my SoulMate.

- I love knowing that no matter what comes between us, we are committed to clearing up misunderstandings and dissolving our ego fears.

What works best and fastest in manifesting a SoulMate is clarity, focus and living as if you are already in relationship with your beloved. When you call to mind and bask in the feeling of being in relationship with your SoulMate on a daily basis, you become irresistible. Imagine waking up in the morning next to your SoulMate. Close your eyes and open your heart right now. How does it feel? You will know you are there when you have a smile on your face.

Or you can say this prayer/greeting:

"Good morning, Beloved! I'm so happy and grateful that you are in my life. You fit my heart so perfectly. I love the support and challenges you bring each day because they arrive on the wings of love. I trust you because I know your life is dedicated to Spirit. It is in and through our relationship with each other that we become clear channels for Divine love in the world. We are together to love each other and serve the world by fulfilling our purpose. The synergy created by our coming together is our unique gift to humanity."

Speaking a message such as this establishes the energetic connection between you and your SoulMate. Once you establish that link, you can rest in the knowledge that you are already connected to your SoulMate and it's only a matter of time before you meet. That perspective fills every new day with a sense of fulfillment.

About three years ago I hosted my first SoulMate MeetUp. I went around the room asking everyone to state as clearly as possible what they wanted in a SoulMate. I remember "Cathy" holding up her Bible and firmly declaring that she wanted a "God-fearing Christian man." She'd come prepared! Yesterday was her engagement party!

YOUR FAIRY GODMOTHER (ALSO) SAYS,
"Choose Consciously"

"If you don't know where you're going, you'll get there. If you don't consciously choose, your unconscious will make the choices for you. Then don't be surprised by what you attract. Also, don't let others choose for you. Don't choose based on a feeling that you should want what others think you should want. That's someone else's preference, not your own. I love this line from Mary Oliver's poem 'Wild Geese': 'You only have to let the soft animal of your body love what it loves.' Go for the yummy!

"Choice isn't about eliminating the wrong things; it's about including the right things. Leave room for surprises. Choose your SoulMate with your soul, not with your ego. Focus on exactly what you want to attract in a SoulMate, not on what you don't want. By the way, there are no wrong choices. There are simply successive approximations, which is a fancy way of saying 'You're getting warmer.'"

Meet Julie

Due to the confidential nature of my work and to protect the privacy of others, I cannot use actual case studies. Instead I have created two characters, Julie and Chuck (whom you will meet in the next chapter), who are composites of family, friends, clients and me, to illustrate how to apply the techniques in this book. Allow me to introduce you!

Julie's Story

Julie, age 32, is a successful attorney. She's following in her father's footsteps and works at his firm. Her father takes great pride in her and is grooming her to take over the firm when he retires.

In her spare time she volunteers for Big Brothers and Big Sisters, and stays fit by going to the gym and practicing yoga at home. She's always wanted to have a child of her own, but her career path has been her top priority. Her friends and dates have mostly come from professional circles. She has very little time to date, but desires a husband and a family.

Julie grew up in a divorced family. She was Daddy's Little Girl and a people pleaser. During high school and college she dated guys she thought Dad would like, but those relationships never resulted in marriage. Dad has never remarried, though he dates a little.

Her friends describe her as driven, successful, intelligent and goal-oriented. In private moments she feels a desire to have less responsibility and someone to share the load with. Her life is full, but doesn't feel satisfying. She's lonely and wants the comforts of family life.

She recently started going back to church in hopes of meeting men who have some depth to them and who are family-oriented. She's had a few dates, but doesn't feel a meaningful connection with any of them. She worries about getting older and wants to have a baby within the next three years. She's beginning to get discouraged. She is hesitant to work with me and cites her hectic schedule as an excuse.

To Julie, her SoulMate would be a man of depth who shares her desire to raise a family based on mutual values and community service.

Inner Work: Ch-ch-ch-ch-Changes

I encourage you to tap along with the examples below. Why? There's a phenomenon that EFT founder Gary Craig calls "borrowing benefits." By tapping along on someone else's issue, you also benefit because the tapping is clearing anything lingering or similar in your energy system at the same time. The reason this works is that there is universality to all human issues. Even though you might not consciously think this is your issue at the time, you might have a related issue. EFT master Carol Look tapped with her clients on their issues and found that her chronic insomnia went away. It was as if her energy system automatically directed the benefits of the tapping to her most bothersome issue.

We are going to work with Julie's issues to demonstrate how she can use EFT to help her commit to manifesting her SoulMate. As Gary Craig says, there are many doors into an issue. We can start anywhere. Julie lacks commitment to manifesting her SoulMate, doesn't make room in her life for her SoulMate and is very vague about what she wants – that is, "a man with depth." She seems more focused on having a baby because at least she has a timeline about that.

Julie is discouraged and hesitant to work with me. That is where we choose to begin. When I ask her to rate the emotional intensity of the following statement: *"I am committed more to my career than to manifesting my SoulMate,"* she says it's an eight "Even though I don't like to admit it."

Therefore we start by tapping on the karate chop point while she repeats the following tapping statement three times aloud and with conviction:

"Even though I am more committed to my career than to manifesting my SoulMate, I deeply love and accept myself."

"Even though I am more committed to my career than to manifesting my SoulMate, I deeply love and accept myself."

"Even though I am more committed to my career than to manifesting my SoulMate, I deeply love and accept myself."

Next we go to the tapping points and tap at least seven times on each point while saying the following tapping phrases:

Top of the Head:	*"I am committed more to my career."*
Inside Eyebrow:	*"I am not committed to manifesting my SoulMate."*
Outside Eyebrow:	*"It's always been like this… since law school."*
Under Eye:	*"I have to get ahead."*
Under Nose:	*"But I'm exhausted."*
Chin:	*"Good thing I'm not meeting any eligible men!"* (Laughs)
Collarbone:	*"I guess I'm not looking very hard."*
Under Arm:	*"Or I'm letting my career be my excuse."*

Top of the Head:	*"I am making excuses."*
Inside Eyebrow:	*"I am actually afraid to meet my SoulMate."*
Outside Eyebrow:	*"My daddy will be disappointed in me."*
Under Eye:	*"Or at least I think so."*
Under Nose:	*"But what if he isn't… and he only wants me to be happy?"*
Chin:	*"Gee, I never thought of that before."* (Laughs)
Collarbone:	*"Maybe I should ask him."* (Sighs)
Under Arm:	*"I'm acting as if something is true when I don't know for sure."*

Top of the Head:	*"I say I want to find my SoulMate, but I'm full of excuses."*
Inside Eyebrow:	*"I am not committed to manifesting my SoulMate."*
Outside Eyebrow:	*"I'm making my daddy the bad guy."*
Under Eye:	*"What if I take responsibility for my life and leave Daddy out of it?"*
Under Nose:	*"I like that idea."*
Chin:	*"But I'm scared without my excuses."*

(Note: Another aspect is appearing here, so I decide to incorporate it into this round of tapping.)

Collarbone:	*"The truth is I don't think I'm going to make a good wife and parent because of my parents' divorce."*

(She rates this fear a 10 on the intensity scale. I make a note that we agree to bring up this fear later in our work.)

Under Arm:	*"I remember how awful that was."*

Top of the Head:	*"I hated their fighting."*
Inside Eyebrow:	*"They put me in the middle."*
Outside Eyebrow:	*"I felt so bad for Daddy."*
Under Eye:	*"I have to be there for him because he was all alone."*
Under Nose:	*"I'm never supposed to leave Daddy alone!"*

(She gasps! Most likely this is a belief that she probably isn't aware she has been harboring… and living by.)

Chin:	*"If I manifest my SoulMate, Daddy will be all alone."*
Collarbone:	*"Or maybe he'll start dating and not be such a workaholic."*
Under Arm:	*"I'm just like my daddy! Oh no!"*

(I note this additional aspect for when it's time to work on releasing past attachments.)

Top of the Head:	*"I would be okay with both of us starting to date and finding our SoulMates."*
Inside Eyebrow:	*"No, I wouldn't!"*
Outside Eyebrow:	*"Yes, I would. (Smiles)"*
Under Eye:	*"NO, I won't!"*
Under Nose:	*"Yes! I WILL!"*
Chin:	*"I could try it and see!"*
Collarbone:	*"What if I just commit to trying and allowing Daddy to do the same?"*
Under Arm:	*"I would be okay with that."*

At this point I stop her and check how intense the original statement feels now:

> *"Even though I am more committed to my career than to manifesting my SoulMate, I deeply love and accept myself."*

She now rates it as a two. "What keeps it at a two?" I ask. "Well, I've had no luck so far," she says. This additional aspect reveals her doubts and fears, which we will address later. I suggest we stick with making a full commitment to manifesting her SoulMate and continue tapping until we get the intensity level of the original statement down to zero. She agrees. So we continue:

Top of the Head:	*"Up until now, I put my career ahead of my SoulMate."*
Inside Eyebrow:	*"I can make a different choice."*
Outside Eyebrow:	*"I am standing in the way of my father finding his SoulMate."* (Tears)
Under Eye:	*"It's time we get out of each other's way."*
Under Nose:	*"This is a gift I give both of us."*

Chin:	*"Maybe this will please my father."*
Collarbone:	*"I know it will please me."* (Sighs)
Under Arm:	*"I allow Daddy to be responsible for his love life while I take responsibility for mine."*

Top of the Head:	*"I commit to finding my SoulMate and allow Daddy to do the same."* (Smiles)
Inside Eyebrow:	*"I can do that!"*
Outside Eyebrow:	*"I can do that!"*
Under Eye:	*"I'm clear now."*
Under Nose:	*"I'm free of my obligation to my father."*
Chin:	*"I am capable of balancing my career with my commitment to manifesting my SoulMate."*
Collarbone:	*"Hurray for me!"* (Grins)
Under Arm:	*"Hurray for me!"*

I stop her again and check how intense the original statement feels now:

"I am committed more to my career than to manifesting my SoulMate."

She now rates it as a zero. Before we leave this issue, we have to test it. I have her close her eyes and focus on the original statement. Using her imagination, I ask her to see if she can get the intensity level to go back up. (I'm looking for other aspects here.) She squints and rolls her head around as if searching for the truth in the old belief. When she opens her eyes, she says, "I don't know why I ever thought I couldn't balance both my career and my personal life. That seems *silly* to me now."

Installation of Desired Beliefs

Once you delete a fear, it is important that you replace it with something. "Nature abhors a vacuum," and will pull something else into that empty slot – probably another fear or unconscious belief. Why not have it be something desirable that you choose – something that you want to manifest?

For Julie, since this is such a difficult issue – one that has so many aspects, *installing* desired beliefs is critical. We selected these beliefs to reinforce and install:

> *"I am capable of balancing my career with my commitment to manifesting my SoulMate."*

> *"I am committed to having my SoulMate."*

> *"I take full responsibility for the success of my love life."*

These are only a few of the affirming statements that Julie (or you) might need. It's a good start. Tap several rounds on each of these statements to install them. Remember to tap in the same way as if you were removing a fear or self-limiting belief.

You might wonder why you can install positive beliefs with EFT by tapping on them and not install or reinforce negative beliefs by tapping on them. The difference is that the negative beliefs are already there. The positive beliefs are not. You tap to *clear* the negative beliefs and tap to *install* positive beliefs.

In these next two exercises, you will create personalized tapping statements and use EFT to create commitment and gain clarity. Being able to do so is the point of this whole book. If you feel scared and think you're unable to do so, tap on *"Even though I don't think I can create tapping statements and use EFT correctly, I deeply love and accept myself."*

Outer Work: Maybe I'm Amazed

In this exercise you will create personalized tapping statements for yourself. Like a Chinese menu, combine one option from the first column with one from the second into a complete tapping statement using the following formula:

"Even though I have been committed to _____ *,* _____ *."*

Select one	Select an ending to the tapping statement
Remaining single	I deeply love and accept myself. (default)
Dating losers	
Dating crazies	
Casual dating	I commit to manifesting my SoulMate instead.
Dating unconsciously	
Playing the field	
My career first	What if a SoulMate relationship is possible anyway?
Casual sex	
One-night stands	
Staying loyal to my ex	I now commit to having exactly what I want.
Being a victim	
Dating fixer-uppers	

Select one	Select an ending to the tapping statement
Dating unavailable people	
My parents/children/friends first	
INSERT FAVORITE "OTHER COMMITMENT" HERE	

Here are examples:

> *"Even though I have been committed to* <u>Remaining single</u>, <u>I now commit to having exactly what I want</u>."

and

> *"Even though I have been committed to* <u>Dating unavailable people</u>, <u>I commit to manifesting my SoulMate instead</u>."

Next rate the intensity level. Then start to tap as instructed in chapter 4. Feel free to adapt some of the tapping phrases from the examples throughout the book for your own use. Continue tapping until your intensity level reaches zero and, after testing, all additional aspects have been cleared.

Outer Work: I Can See Clearly Now

In this exercise you will create personalized tapping statements for yourself. Like a Chinese menu, combine one option from the first column with one from the second into a complete tapping statement using the following formula:

"Even though I don't YET know _____ *,*
_____ *."*

Select one	Select an ending to the tapping statement
What I want	I deeply love and accept myself. (default)
Who I want	
How I want to be	What if I do know deep down?
What I have to give	
How to pick good people	I choose to know now.
How to get clear	
How I want to feel	I know what I want to feel.
What I deserve	
What's lovable about me	I trust the part of me that does know.
What I need to do differently	
What I want to receive	I allow it to be revealed.
What my deal-breakers are	
The difference between what I want and what I need	I allow my SoulMate to come to me anyhow.
INSERT FAVORITE "NOT KNOWING" HERE	

Here are examples:

> *"Even though I don't YET know* <u>What I want, I allow my SoulMate to come to me anyhow."</u>

and

> *"Even though I don't YET know* <u>How to get clear, I trust the part of me that does know."</u>

Next rate the intensity level. Then start to tap as instructed in chapter 4. Feel free to adapt some of the tapping phrases from the examples throughout the book for your own use. Continue tapping until your intensity level reaches zero and, after testing, all additional aspects have been cleared.

What's Next?

In chapter 6 you will learn how to identify and start clearing the conscious and unconscious impediments to manifesting your SoulMate.

Chapter 6
IDENTIFY THE IMPEDIMENTS;
ENTER THE CAVE

"The cave you fear to enter holds the treasure you seek."

JOSEPH CAMPBELL

HOW MANY SELF-HELP books have you read on dating, relationships, love and finding the right partner? Many of my clients come in with armfuls of books and throw them at my feet in frustration. "This doesn't work!" When I ask if they've actually applied what they learned in the books, I get mixed responses. One of the things that I've gleaned from my 23+ years in mental health and coaching is that people fear looking within; they are afraid of what they will find there. They are even more fearful of taking responsibility for the results they get in their lives – even when they are miserable or lonely. Most people are terrified of this power – of being accountable for their own lives. While desiring change, they are simultaneously afraid of change – afraid of dropping the old paradigms that do not work in their lives. They like to read about attracting a SoulMate, but resist doing the work – all the while protesting that they want their lives to be different.

This is why *inner work* is now being called the *final frontier* – because it is the ultimate confrontation with the unknown. We fear what is lurking below our carefully crafted personas. We fear and project onto others both our strengths and our shadow. However, as Campbell says above, the unknown is also the source of our treasure. When you do your inner work, remove the impediments found there and shift your beliefs so that you are in alignment with your SoulMate, the treasures show up.

It's almost a rule of nature that once you gain clarity and commit to manifesting something into your life, the first things that arise are the fears and doubts. I like to say "Right on time!" when that happens. It is not something to be discouraged about, though it is unpleasant to experience. One good thing about fears and doubts is that you have an emotional and physical reaction to them that easily gets your attention. Those intense feelings are signs that you are in the grip of something that needs your attention – and your intention – to heal.

It is a whole other thing to identify what is going on unconsciously. That is like asking a fish to be aware of the water it lives in. We take our worldview and beliefs for granted. We think our worldview is normal and that everybody shares our beliefs about reality. We don't consciously realize that there are an infinite number of ways to view the world and infinite worlds to experience. Your current worldview, which doesn't include your SoulMate, is what is manifesting. A shift in consciousness needs to take place that *collapses* the wave of infinite possibilities (as quantum theorists say) into the reality of the SoulMate your life needs.

Making the Unconscious Conscious

> *"Until you make the unconscious conscious, it will direct your life and you will call it fate."*

> CARL JUNG

The way the world appears to you mirrors what you believe on both conscious and unconscious levels. Each aspect of your life, including your love life, reflects your accumulated unconscious beliefs and projected shadow aspects. If you believe that there is no one out there for you or that you are not worthy of love and commitment, that will be reflected in your outer experience. If you project all your neediness onto others, those will be the people you continually attract. Instead of seeing that as something you can change, you agree with what Jung says above and call it fate.

The nature of the unconscious is its mystery and invisibility. Its contents are outside of our usual awareness, therefore hard to detect directly. You can readily report on the contents of your conscious mind if you stop to notice what you are thinking, but you cannot do the same with the unconscious. Since the unconscious is, well… unconscious, you have to learn to speak its language, interpret its signs and notice how it manifests in your life. In that way it is like the wind or gravity. You know it is there because you can see the effects of it, but you can't observe it directly.

The unconscious mind is:

- visual, yet concrete. It thinks in pictures. You have to tell it
  what you desire by describing a picture or scene that a five-year-
  old would understand. Include all your senses in crafting the
  description.

- faster in processing information than the conscious mind. It takes
  in a lot of information and gives it back to you in the form of
  reactions, hunches, intuition or dreams.

- the repository of all your life experiences, memories, shadow
  aspects, things you've learned or concluded and decisions you've
  made as a result.

- associative. It bundles things together that seem the same, such as situations that have the same tone of feeling, like the hurt, sadness or disappointment when getting rejected.

- able to be aligned with consciously chosen goals, desires and dreams.

- in charge of your life. It is what makes your body breathe, digest, eliminate, move, react to threat and heal without your having to think about it.

There are four ways to identify unconscious impediments:

- Look for recurring themes from past relationships.

- Determine the underlying beliefs that lead to fear and doubt.

- Free-associate to words like *love, dating, commitment, marriage, sex* and *intimacy*

- Become aware of projected shadow aspects

You did the first two of these steps in earlier exercises in the book. Hopefully you are already working diligently to create tapping statements and using EFT to successfully clear these fears and beliefs.

Projecting Your Shadow onto Others: It's Not Them. It's You.

If what makes you irritable, frustrated and rejecting of others is your projected shadow aspects, how can you acknowledge them and claim the power contained within them? How can you coax the unconscious shadow to reveal itself? How can you see your blindspots? As much as we want to disown the shadow or may be horrified by what we find lurking there, being willing to look for and acknowledge it is a good start.

If this is such horrifying work, why would you want to do this? Psychologist David Richo says, "As we bring our dark side into the light, we feel a kinship with all beings – a giant step towards love." Shadow work is empowering and freeing. It allows you to stop projecting your negative aspects onto others, which in turn frees you from continually manifesting that type of person. The only reason you attract people with negative qualities is that you haven't yet learned the lesson and accepted that you also carry the seeds of these characteristics in yourself.

Here's how one of my SoulMate ManiFest students, "Vicki," worked through her shadow:

"We were doing a 'shadow self' exercise in class last night. I was saying, 'I am committed to waiting for someone to fix/love me.' The phrase morphed to an emphasis on *waiting* and left out *fix*. So there my partner and I were, saying back and forth, 'I am committed to waiting for someone to love me.' After a while it became apparent that I was committed to *waiting*. Then we switched to 'I used to be committed to waiting for someone to love me, and now I am committed to *being* my most loving self. I do this for myself and I love the way it benefits others as well.' I began to cry. I had thought I was already on board with loving myself, but it appears there is more to learn, to do and to know. Then I began to journal on ideas for being more loving to myself.

"Another big moment of clarity for me was meeting and understanding the needy little girl who lives inside me. Perhaps now that I know she's a part of me, I will not be blindsided by her – my – neediness. In fact, I now see how 'Little Vicki' is actually helping me by wanting to be heard and valued. Now 'Big Victoria' can consciously choose to be in relationship with a man who hears and values her. In the past I have settled. I felt I was only lovable when I was helping another... and of course that means I attracted needy men for me to help. *No more!* Now I am actively seeking someone who doesn't need me, but who values me... who enjoys being with me... whose life I enrich just by virtue of being *me*. I now move away from emotional caretaking and into emotional, mental and physical sharing. Love it!"

People pay therapists thousands of dollars to help them identify what is in their shadow. I am also a therapist, so I am going to give you the cheat sheet.

Among the following statements you will surely find at least a few that anger or insult you. If so, you have stumbled upon a gold mine. Those statements are where you have some work to do. To empower yourself to have exactly what you want in your current or future relationships, *own* the disowned parts of yourself instead of *dating* them.

Note in your journal the statements below that apply to you. You can tell by reading each statement. The ones that evoke a strong emotional reaction, especially of denial or repulsion, indicate what is hiding in your shadow. Each of these can be turned into a tapping statement in order to claim the power hidden in them. This is not an exhaustive list. Once you get the idea, you will notice how and when you project your shadow in your daily interactions with people. Here we go:

If you attract partners who use and abuse you, it's because you don't know what you deserve.

If you attract partners who can't commit, it's because you are not truly committed to having what you want.

If you attract partners who suck the life out of you, it's because you don't have strong boundaries.

If you attract partners who are controlling, it's because you are addicted to playing the victim.

If you attract partners who cheat, it's because you are not willing to be fully present.

If you attract partners who tolerate your cheating, it's because you have a fear of intimacy.

If you attract partners who are untrustworthy, it's because you don't trust your gut or listen to yourself.

If you attract partners who are fixer-uppers, it's because you avoid or deny your own needs.

If you attract partners who are addicted to food, sex, work or drugs, it's because you are co-dependent.

If you attract partners who are needy and clingy, it's because you discount and deny your own needs.

If you attract partners who are always trying to change you, it's because you avoid full responsibility for your life.

If you attract partners who only deal in superficialities, it's because you haven't plumbed your own depths.

If you attract partners who want to rescue you, it's because you haven't rescued yourself.

If you attract partners who are takers, it's because you are addicted to people-pleasing and blaming.

If you attract partners who criticize and berate you, it's because you have hidden guilt and are in need of self-forgiveness.

If you attract partners whom you can never please, it's because you aren't pleasing yourself.

If you attract partners who want only sex, it's because you haven't mastered the art of negotiation.

If you attract partners who are silent, it's because you are afraid of others' thoughts, feelings and needs.

If you attract partners who are passive and can't make decisions, it's because you have a need to always be in control.

If you attract partners who steal your money and possessions, it's because you trust untrustworthy people.

If you attract partners who aren't turned on by you, it's because you don't value or respect your sexuality.

If you attract partners who avoid conflicts, it's because you don't want to know who they really are or show who you really are.

If you attract partners who are rage-aholics, it's because you fear and deny your own rage.

If you attract partners who are boring, it's because you aren't in touch with your own aliveness and creativity.

If you attract partners who are immature, it's either because you want to parent them or you want a playmate.

If you attract partners who demean you, it's because you have low self-esteem.

If you attract partners who are cold and unaffectionate, it's because you don't allow warmth and closeness.

If you attract partners who are "bad boys," it's because you need to rebel.

If you attract partners who are "too good" for you by virtue of some amazing talent or personal strength, it's because you haven't developed that in yourself.

Go back to chapter 2 and look at the list of traits and characteristics emerging from your past-love stories. These will tell you what is in your shadow. Fill in the blanks in the following statement with the characteristics and traits of past loves: *"I am attracted to people who are _____, therefore I need to claim _____ in myself."* Then you can turn each of these into a tapping statement. For example, *"Even though I deny and project my 'emotional unavailability' onto my dates, I deeply love and forgive myself for my own emotional unavailability."*

Until you have claimed these shadow aspects in yourself, you will manifest people who will carry your shadow aspects for you. The most likely response to being with someone like that is attempting to change *them*. You can't change them, but you can empower yourself through claiming and integrating the hidden power within your shadow. Then who you attract will change. By claiming the power of your projections, you become more personally powerful. You also put yourself in alignment with your SoulMate when you don't look for them to be "better" or "worse" than you. You can then be magnificently, tragically and ultimately human, and love each other warts and all.

"Susy" had a history of attracting emotionally unavailable partners. After learning to use EFT to clear other fears and barriers, she worked on this tapping statement at home: *"Even though I attract emotionally unavailable partners, I deeply love and forgive myself."* In the course of tapping several rounds to reduce the intensity level from a six to a zero, Susy discovered that by attracting these types she could play the victim and deny her fears of intimacy and commitment. This realization opened up a softer side of herself, allowed her to take more emotional risks and revealed more about herself in a developing relationship. She was pleased to report how people seemed warmer and reciprocated with more personal sharing as well.

YOUR FAIRY GODMOTHERS SAYS,
"Take That Back!"

"Remember what author Marianne Williamson said: 'Our deepest fear is not that we are inadequate. Our deepest fear is that we are powerful beyond measure.' This applies to you, too. She wasn't talking about 'other people.' She was talking about you.

"The way you become powerful is to make the unconscious conscious and reclaim your shadow. Huh? It's a fancy way of saying 'Know thyself' – including all the things you want to deny. Taking back your projections makes you whole. When you are whole, you are holy. When you are whole and holy you are following your life's purpose. You are walking the path of destiny... that, coincidentally, leads right to your SoulMate."

Meet Chuck

Chuck is 42 years old, divorced and living alone. His last significant relationship with Pamela lasted four years. He assumed it was going to last forever, but she never would commit to him. About two years ago she broke it off to "explore starting a second career." They remain friends, but this mostly consists of Chuck doing favors for Pamela. He dates occasionally, but always breaks up once the woman puts any demands on him, especially for more than friendship.

Chuck works as an art teacher at a junior high school in an affluent suburb. To supplement his teacher's salary, he freelances as a wedding photographer and sells his art through galleries and art fairs. Always alert for an opportunity to get ahead, Chuck lost money in some investments and MLM marketing schemes that did not work out.

Chuck doesn't speak much about his early life or marriage. When he does, it's only in very general terms. Of his marriage all he says is, "things were fine until she went crazy." He has two daughters from that marriage, Ashley, age 21, and Stephanie, age 14. Chuck is closest to Stephanie, who lives with his ex-wife. He's had a hard time with this since the divorce because he does not have full custody of her and cannot protect her. The decision was mostly financial. His ex makes more money and handles it more responsibly than he does.

Chuck's parents are elderly but remain happily married despite many financial and health challenges. Chuck sees them once or twice a year and calls his mom on Sunday afternoons each week.

Chuck was sexually abused as a youth by a teen minister. He has never revealed it to anyone. His father was an Evangelical Christian minister in that same church and was friends with this teen minister. When Chuck was 14, his father quit the ministry to work for Ford in Lima, Ohio, in order to support his growing family. Chuck was relieved, after moving away, that his father was no longer associated with the teen minister through that church, but very angry at God. To cope with feelings of shame and disgust, Chuck drinks a little more than he should.

Friends describe Chuck as hard to get to know, a bit of a control freak, and somewhat lost. Chuck wonders if he is damaged and incapable of having successful relationships with women. He would like to have a relationship like his parents have that lasts forever even when there are challenges present. To Chuck, his SoulMate would be someone who accepts him as he is, helps him heal his underlying shame and shares his passion for art and photography.

Inner Work: Man in the Mirror

In the following exercises you will learn how to work with any projected shadow aspect. You will tap along with 42-year-old divorced Chuck. His marriage was "fine until she went crazy." This is a clear statement of Chuck's projecting his own craziness onto his ex-wife. Maybe you've dated or were married to a crazy and can relate. As before, you are encouraged to borrow benefits by tapping along with Chuck for the following tapping statement:

"Even though I attract crazies because I deny my own craziness, I deeply love and accept myself."

As always, start by determining the intensity level for the tapping statement, where zero = no intensity and ten = the most intensity you can imagine. Since Chuck is in such deep denial, he rates it a 10. He is convinced his ex-wife was the crazy and he had nothing to do with that. He might be a tough nut to crack!

Begin, as always, tapping on the karate chop point and repeating the entire tapping statement three times aloud and with conviction:

"Even though I attract crazies because I deny my own craziness, I deeply love and accept myself."

"Even though I attract crazies because I deny my own craziness, I deeply love and accept myself."

"Even though I attract crazies because I deny my own craziness, I deeply love and accept myself."

Next Chuck taps at least seven times on each of the following tapping points while repeating the following tapping phrases:

Head:	*"I attract crazies…"*
Inside Eyebrow:	*"My ex-wife went crazy."*
Outside Eyebrow:	*"That's why we are divorced."*
Under Eye:	*"That's the ONLY reason we got divorced."*
Nose:	*"Because she went crazy."*
Chin:	*"Things were fine for a long time."*
Collarbone:	*"Or so I thought."*
Under Arm:	*"Then she went crazy."*

Head:	*"I was attracted a crazy woman…"*
Inside Eyebrow:	*"And didn't know it."*
Outside Eyebrow:	*"Why did I need to do that?"*
Under Eye:	*"I needed a crazy woman…"*
Nose:	*"So I could focus on her…"*
Chin:	*"Blame her…"*
Collarbone:	*"Take the spotlight off me."*
Under Arm:	*"I could fade into the background…"*

Head:	*"Be the long suffering husband…"*
Inside Eyebrow:	*"Get a lot of sympathy…"*
Outside Eyebrow:	*"Feel good about myself…"*
Under Eye:	*"Never have to focus on my own craziness."*
Nose:	*"My own craziness…"*
Chin:	*"That I couldn't face…"*
Collarbone:	*"Way too painful…"*
Under Arm:	*"Hidden from me."*

Head:	*"I'd rather be divorced than crazy."*
Inside Eyebrow:	*"Rather be divorced than examine my craziness."*
Outside Eyebrow:	*"Blame her…"*
Under Eye:	*"Not take any responsibility for my part in it."*
Nose:	*"No one blames me."*

Chin:	*"I can't blame me."*
Collarbone:	*"I don't want to know about my own craziness."*
Under Arm:	*"Even though I've always known it's there."*

Head:	*"I am invested in NOT dealing with it."*
Inside Eyebrow:	*"Easier to deal with someone else's craziness."* (Gasps!)
Outside Eyebrow:	*"But what about my craziness?"*
Under Eye:	*"I don't want to attract another crazy woman."*
Nose:	*"Yes, I do."*
Chin:	*"No, I don't."*
Collarbone:	*"I might need to in order to run from my own craziness."*
Under Arm:	*"I am running from my own craziness."* (Yawns)

Head:	*"I'm not crazy."*
Inside Eyebrow:	*"I'm afraid I'm crazy."*
Outside Eyebrow:	*"I am really afraid I'm crazy."*
Under Eye:	*"What if I have my own craziness to deal with?"*
Nose:	*"Can I face that?"*
Chin:	*After all these years, can I own up to my own problems?"*
Collarbone:	*"Maybe…"*
Under Arm:	*"Maybe not."*

Head:	*"Nobody's perfect…"*
Inside Eyebrow:	*"Including me"*
Outside Eyebrow:	*"Nobody's perfect…"*
Under Eye:	*"Including me."* (Sighs)
Nose:	*"Maybe I, too, have a crazy side…"*
Chin:	*"That contributed to my divorce."*
Collarbone:	*"Maybe my crazy side…"*
Under Arm:	*"Drove my ex-wife crazy."* (Laughs)

Head:	*"Okay, so maybe I drove her crazy…"*
Inside Eyebrow:	*"Because of something in me that I didn't deal with."*
Outside Eyebrow:	*"No, I didn't!"*
Under Eye:	*"Yes, I did."*
Nose:	*"I don't want to believe this."*
Chin:	*"But I am willing to consider it."* (Sighs)
Collarbone:	*"I am willing to consider it…"*
Under Arm:	*"Because I don't want to go through THAT again!"*

It's time to check in with Chuck. His intensity level started at a 10. He's now at a four and willing to consider how his own unconscious, unexamined craziness contributed to his marriage ending up in divorce. We decide to continue with this modified tapping statement, which he repeats aloud and with conviction three times while tapping on the karate chop point:

> *"Even though I attracted a crazy so I could deny my own craziness, I deeply love and accept myself."*

> *"Even though I attracted a crazy so I could deny my own craziness, I deeply love and accept myself."*

> *"Even though I attracted a crazy so I could deny my own craziness, I deeply love and accept myself."*

Go back to the tapping points and continue tapping at least seven times on the following tapping phrases:

Head:	*"I attracted a crazy woman so I could deny my own craziness."*
Inside Eyebrow:	*"Boy, was I smart!"*
Outside Eyebrow:	*"I kept the focus off myself for years."*

Under Eye: *"Until I was ready to deal with it."*
Nose: *"I kept the focus off myself for years."*
Chin: *"And now I'm ready to deal with it."*
Collarbone: *"No, I'm not."*
Under Arm: *"Yes, I am."*

Head: *"No, I'm not."*
Inside Eyebrow: *"Maybe I am."* (Sighs)
Outside Eyebrow: *"Okay, maybe there's something to this."*
Under Eye: *"Maybe I did contribute something…"*
Nose: *"That I just didn't want to see or deal with."*
Chin: *"Until now…"*
Collarbone: *"I wasn't ready before."*
Under Arm: *"I'm not sure I'm ready now."*

Head: *"But I am sure that I want someone who…"*
Inside Eyebrow: *"Accepts me for who I am…"*
Outside Eyebrow: *"All of who I am…"*
Under Eye: *"Good and bad."*
Nose: *"Guess I'd better accept myself first."*
Chin: *"Good and bad."*
Collarbone: *"How can I expect someone else to…"*
Under Arm: *"If I don't fully know and accept myself?"*

Head: *"I really want someone who accepts me fully."*
Inside Eyebrow: *"Starting with me."*
Outside Eyebrow: *"Starting with me."* (Chokes up)
Under Eye: *"I don't accept myself…"*
Nose: *"Yet."*
Chin: *"I am learning to accept myself…"*
Collarbone: *"All of myself…"*
Under Arm: *"Good and bad."*

Head:	*"I choose to accept my own craziness..."*
Inside Eyebrow:	*"Love and forgive myself..."*
Outside Eyebrow:	*"Love and forgive myself..."*
Under Eye:	*"For being human..."*
Nose:	*"For doing what I needed to..."*
Chin:	*"To survive until I got strong enough..."*
Collarbone:	*"To deal with my own craziness."*
Under Arm:	*"The bad things that happened to me..."*

Head:	*"That I wanted to bury..."*
Inside Eyebrow:	*"And blame others for..."*
Outside Eyebrow:	*"And pretend I wasn't hurt..."*
Under Eye:	*"Or affected in any way."*
Nose:	*"I tried so hard to be normal..."*
Chin:	*"That I ruined my marriage."*
Collarbone:	*"I had a part in this..."*
Under Arm:	*"Not all of it, but I did have my part."*

Head:	*"I didn't want to deal with my own craziness..."*
Inside Eyebrow:	*"So I drove her crazy."*
Outside Eyebrow:	*"It took years to do it..."*
Under Eye:	*"But I prevailed!"* (Laughs)
Nose:	*"I don't know whether to laugh or cry..."*
Chin:	*"Laugh or cry..."*
Collarbone:	*"Maybe I drove my ex-wife crazy..."*
Under Arm:	*"So I didn't have to face some truths about myself."* (Sighs)

Head:	*"There were things about my past..."*
Inside Eyebrow:	*"That I just wasn't ready to face."*
Outside Eyebrow:	*"She didn't know about them..."*
Under Eye:	*"But they affected her..."*

Nose:	*"They affected us."* (Yawns)
Chin:	*"It's time to clear those things…"*
Collarbone:	*"So I can accept myself for ALL of who I am…"*
Under Arm:	*"And attract someone who will do so, too."* (Smiles)

It's time to check in and see how intense the tapping statement feels for Chuck right now. He now says it's at zero. So I have Chuck test to see if he can make the intensity go back up. He closes his eyes and repeats the original tapping statement quietly to himself to notice what happens. When he opens his eyes, he says, "I have to apologize to my ex-wife! I didn't see this about myself. I so wanted it to be solely about her… her fault. I didn't want to look at my past and all the dark things that happened to me. I just wanted to shut it away. Now I see that I was so focused on her craziness… it was actually a relief… because I was running away from my past."

Installation of Desired Beliefs

For Chuck this was a crucial, glaring issue. Once the shadow aspect is removed, it is vital to install desired beliefs to replace it. We selected these beliefs to reinforce and install:

"I am loveable in all my humanness – warts and all."

"I accept myself and ALL of who I am."

"I attract people who accept me just the way I am."

These are only a few of the affirming statements that Chuck (or you) might need. It's a good start. Tap several rounds on each of these statements to install them. Remember to tap in the same way you would if you were removing a fear or self-limiting belief.

Outer Work: Who's Bad?

In this exercise you will create personalized tapping statements for yourself. Like a Chinese menu, combine one option from the first column with one from the second into a complete tapping statement using the following formula:

"Even though I can't stand _____ *in others,*
_____.*"*

Select one	Select an ending to the tapping statement
Entitlement	I deeply love and accept myself. (default)
Anger	
Inability to commit	
Cheating	I know that I am not perfect.
Lying	
Neediness/Clinginess	
Dominance	I see some of that in myself.
Submissiveness	
Superficiality	
Coldness	I use that part of myself at select times.
Withholding	
Passivity	

Select one	Select an ending to the tapping statement
Aggressiveness	I extract the power in that quality for myself and use it for good.
Immaturity	
Pride	
INSERT FAVORITE "TURN OFF" HERE	

Here are examples:

"Even though I can't stand <u>Immaturity</u> *in others,* <u>I claim and love that in myself, too.</u> *"*

and

"Even though I can't stand <u>Lying</u> *in others,* <u>I extract the power in that quality for myself and use it for good.</u>*

Write yours below:

Next rate the intensity level. Then start to tap as instructed in chapter 4. Feel free to adapt some of the tapping phrases from the examples throughout the book for your own use. Continue tapping until your intensity level reaches zero and, after testing, all additional aspects have been cleared.

BONUS #1: *Free Association, Clustering and Mind Mapping*

Free association is a technique by which you quickly and without a lot of conscious thought list everything that comes to mind when presented with a word or idea. You can take what you uncover in this exercise and turn it into tapping statements.

Clustering, which is very similar to brainstorming and mind mapping, is a visual free-association exercise that starts with a central word or concept. Lines and circles connect concepts to the core word. The goal of this exercise is to get at your conscious and unconscious associations with a particular word or concept.

To do this exercise, get six blank sheets of paper and write one of the following words in the middle of each page:

- Love
- Marriage
- Dating
- SoulMate
- Commitment

Write down all your thoughts and feelings associated with each word. You can do it with lines creating a spider web of associations, or get a mind mapping application online, like Mind Meister, XMind or FreeMind to create a visual layout of your thoughts and ideas. (See http://lifehacker. com/5188833/hive-five-five-best-mind-mapping-applications.)

Work quickly to get maximum results. You might notice that you have both positive and negative associations with any word. Those negative associations are what are blocking you from manifesting your SoulMate. Once you have this list compiled, ask yourself, "How might this belief/fear/experience/expectation block my SoulMate from showing up in my life?" Then create your unique tapping statements like the example below.

BONUS! Overcome Limiting Beliefs about Love

"Even though I think love is _____,
_____."

Select one or two at the most	Select an ending to the tapping statement
Scary	I deeply love and accept myself.
Painful	
Frustrating	I want it anyhow.
Sad	
Hard to find	What if I look for the gift in this?
Non-existent	
Embarrassing	What if this was just a fluke?
Damaging	
Confusing	I welcome a better experience in the future.
Distressing	
Bittersweet	I choose to tell myself a different story now.
Rare	
A form of insanity	What if all the good stuff is ahead for me?
A joke	
Not in the cards for me	What if all the bad stuff is behind me?
INSERT YOUR "EMOTION OR BELIEF" HERE	

Next: Like a Chinese menu, create your unique tapping statement by combining one option from the first column with one from the second. For example:

> *"Even though I think love is* <u>A form of insanity,</u> <u>I welcome a better</u> <u>experience in the future.</u> *"*

or

> *"Even though I think love is* <u>Hard to find,</u> <u>I choose to tell myself a different</u> <u>story now."</u>

Next rate the intensity level. Then start to tap as instructed in chapter 4. Feel free to adapt some of the tapping phrases from the examples throughout the book for your own use. Continue tapping until your intensity level reaches zero and, after testing, all additional aspects have been cleared.

What's Next?

In chapter 7 you will learn to use EFT to eliminate paralyzing fears and replace them with positive expectations. This will allow you to take inspired action, live your purpose and manifest your SoulMate. Though facing fear is not for the faint of heart, you can now use EFT as the fear eradicator. This makes you more confident in taking risks and stretching outside of your comfort zone.

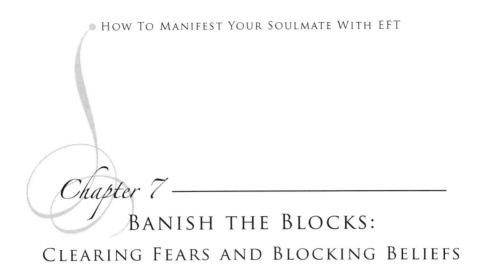

Chapter 7

BANISH THE BLOCKS:
CLEARING FEARS AND BLOCKING BELIEFS

"Love is letting go of fear."

GERALD JAMPOLSKY

LET'S FACE IT. Fear is paralyzing. It blocks good things, situations and people from manifesting into your life. Sometimes people think that they will just wait until they are no longer fearful before doing something they desire, like:

- asking someone out on a date

- risking their heart

- making a commitment to a long-term relationship

The trouble is that dreams die in the waiting. Opportunities are missed. What's worse is that waiting never makes the fear go away. In fact, when you focus on and ruminate about fearful thoughts, they multiply! In this case, time doesn't heal all. Action is required.

Fear is a belief in our own powerlessness and in the possibility of bad things happening in the future. Except for when we are in actual physical danger, fear is simply the "awfulizing," "what if" thoughts about an imaginary future that we play over and over in our heads. I don't know who coined it, but someone said FEAR = False Expectations Appearing Real. We tend to believe fearful thoughts are the truth just because our physical and emotional reactions to them are so strong. This is nonsense. It is important to make a distinction between intense feelings and accurate perceptions. Most people don't. Instead what we do is focus more and more on the thought until we can't stand it, act out of the fear or flee the situation altogether. Good things seldom follow such actions.

When you act on fearful thoughts and beliefs, they become self-fulfilling. In the realm of relationships, if you have a fear of rejection you will create the thing you fear in unconscious ways. Then you can say, "See! I told you this was true!" For example, you might have a fear of being smothered. This fear leads you to perceive any contact from the person you're dating as needy, therefore evidence of your belief. "See! Look, she can't even go three days without talking to me."

In my practice, it is common to see anxious and fearful people avoid situations that trigger their fears. Sometimes they project their fears and beliefs onto others. I remember a middle-aged client who was frustrated with dating. To deal with his fear of rejection, he developed a façade of not caring. He also believed women wanted "bad boys." Of course this didn't make him very attractive to the women he was interested in. Deep down he really wanted a connection. However, to be open and genuine was too vulnerable. What he would do unconsciously to confirm his fear was to select women he thought of as unattainable. He then treated them with thinly veiled contempt and distain. When they ignored him he reacted with anger, sometimes telling them off.

When other women expressed interest in him, he was not receptive. They weren't pretty/thin/interesting enough for him. He would hang out for a while with them, all the while looking for an infraction so he would have a reason to reject them. Ultimately he would reject them before they rejected him. His behavior reminded me of this Groucho Marx quote: "I wouldn't want to belong to any club that would have me as a member." My client was trapped in a dating cycle that confirmed his worst fears and shaky self-esteem.

Fear is a signal that you are at your emotional frontier. Being able to recognize when you are caught up in fearful thoughts is a start. Being able to rid yourself of them altogether is the goal. As Marianne Williams says, "Love is what we were born with. Fear is what we have learned here." I like to say that the proper response to fearful thoughts is "Liar, liar, pants on fire!"

Love and fear cannot coexist. Fear is the ego masquerading as wisdom. If you listen to it, your world will shrink. People who are afraid don't take risks or try new things. What you desire is on the other side of fear. In short, fear stands between you and your SoulMate.

When you remove fears, the natural essence of who you are – love – shines a beacon for your SoulMate, guiding them to you. Without fear your heart is abundant in love, kindness and compassion because it is no longer hampered by those chains.

It is not easy to calm down if you are in the grip of fear. It feels like your emotions have disabled the logical side of your brain and you are on a runaway train bound for disaster. This is where meditation, another technique for reducing fear and anxiety, can help. Meditation brings you into the "now." In the present moment your mind simply notes or notices your thoughts with detachment. It is as if you've gotten off of the "train" of your thoughts, stepped back several yards, and can simply watch them pass by.

Meditation takes a long time to master, however. That is why I like EFT. It can be learned in 10 minutes. EFT is amazingly effective for reducing or eliminating fears altogether and installing positive beliefs and expectations. It is a tool that empowers you to move forward and create, nurture and sustain the kind of loving relationships you seek.

After identifying a fear of rejection from having a cold and uncaring family life while she was growing up, one of my clients went home and tapped about this specific issue. Without help from me, she reported that not only did she clear her fear, but when testing to see if she could make the fear come back, she thought it was ridiculous to call anything "rejection" if the person didn't really know her in the first place. This gave her courage to approach someone in whom she was interested for a date.

What You Believe Is What You See

> *"Man, alone, has the power to transform his thoughts into physical reality; man, alone, can dream and make his dreams come true."*

> NAPOLEON HILL

Success authors such as Napoleon Hill, Jim Rohn, Tony Robbins and Jack Canfield talk about the tremendous power of your beliefs to influence the future, but they don't tell you how to change those beliefs quickly and easily. That is where I have found EFT to be tremendously powerful. It is a quick way to remove old, self-defeating beliefs and install new, life-affirming beliefs.

We act on what we believe. Therefore it is crucial to examine and replace beliefs that do not assist you in manifesting your SoulMate. Your SoulMate might already be in your life, but you cannot see them because you have a belief that they would not be interested in you. Likewise, if you believe that you are unattractive, you might discount (or not even notice) people flirting with you.

The relationship between beliefs, feelings and actions is a closed loop. What you think influences how you feel. What you feel influences how you behave. How you behave influences what you think. It is cyclic. To transform yourself into a person who manifests your SoulMate, it is abso-lutely vital to develop the ability to crack open this loop and replace old, self-limiting beliefs about yourself, others and the way the world works.

Here is a success story from one of my students:

"During Annette's SoulMate ManiFest class, we learned EFT and I found it extremely useful in working on specific issues related to love, dating, sex, marriage, and commitment. EFT helped me identify the unconscious beliefs that were keeping me from finding a partner. My biggest barrier was the belief that being close to someone meant I'd lose myself and my freedom, something that had happened in all my previous relationships.

"I am happy to report that I met my current boyfriend shortly after completing the course. This is the healthiest relationship I have ever been in. I have been able to stay true to myself as well as maintain my freedom. I believe EFT helped me remove the blocks in my body's energy system as well as heal my negative beliefs regarding relationships."

YOUR FAIRY GODMOTHER SAYS, *"Don't Believe Everything You Think"*

"Honey, you already know that you don't want to believe half the things you think, and certainly none of the things that fearful inner voice tells you. Let's just clear that up right now. Fear never tells you the truth. If, however, you hold on to it, you will make the thing you fear come true. I've seen it over and over again. It's sad, really. Your fear becomes a self-fulfilling prophesy. Not because it is true, but because thinking makes it so.

"*How to Manifest Your SoulMate with EFT* gives you tools to rid yourself of fears. Use them – unless you like living in a state of fear and paralysis. Hey! You could even tap about that: '*Even though I like living in a state of fear and paralysis, I deeply love and accept myself.*' Get with the program!

"Honestly, fearful people are boring and not much fun to be around. How are you going to manifest a wonderful SoulMate if you're trapped by fear? You're not. It is as simple as that.

"Yes, there is a SoulMate out there for you. If you don't believe that, you won't manifest the one you desire. I know you have been waiting a long time; you might be steeped in doubt. Hold fast to the idea that your SoulMate is moving in your direction. Unwavering certainty will help bring it about."

Inner Work: I Think I'm Scared of What the Future Holds

Remember Julie, whom you met in chapter 5? Julie is a people pleaser. Her main fear is that there is no one who will satisfy both her desires and those of her father. She can't imagine that there is anyone out there for her. This fear paralyzes or sabotages the relationships she forms. If she doesn't believe that there's anyone out there for her, why would she keep trying?

We decide to work on this fear. The tapping statement is:

"Even though I am afraid that there's no one out there for me, I deeply love and accept myself."

The intensity level for this fear is a seven in the present moment. If this is one of your fears too, or even if it is not, tap along to borrow the benefits.

Begin by tapping on the karate chop point while repeating aloud and with conviction:

"Even though I am afraid that there's no one out there for me, I deeply love and accept myself."

"Even though I am afraid that there's no one out there for me, I deeply love and accept myself."

"Even though I am afraid that there's no one out there for me, I deeply love and accept myself."

Next go to the tapping points. Tap at least seven times on each point while saying the following tapping phrases:

Head:	*"There's no one out there for me."*
Inside Eyebrow:	*"There's no one out there for me."*
Outside Eyebrow:	*"I am preoccupied with this fear."*
Under Eye:	*"It consumes all my energy."*
Nose:	*"I feel defeated before I start."* (Sighs)
Chin:	*"I am defeated before I start."*
Collarbone:	*"Because I think there's no one out there for me…"*
Under Arm:	*"So why try?"*

Head:	*"Why put my best out there?"*
Inside Eyebrow:	*"Why risk being vulnerable?"*
Outside Eyebrow:	*"Why keep meeting new people?"*
Under Eye:	*"Only to get my hopes dashed again…"*
Nose:	*"And again."*
Chin:	*"I don't know how much more I can take."*
Collarbone:	*"I feel like giving up…"* (Sighs)
Under Arm:	*"Maybe I'm just meant to be alone."*

Head:	*"But what if I'm not?"*
Inside Eyebrow:	*"Do I want to give up already?"*

Outside Eyebrow:	*"What if my SoulMate is the next person I meet?"*
Under Eye:	*"What if my SoulMate is the next person I meet?"* (Yawns)
Nose:	*"I'd certainly regret giving up."*
Chin:	*"Even though this is all hard…"*
Collarbone:	*"Maybe it's worth it…"*
Under Arm:	*"To finally meet my SoulMate."*
Head:	*"I guess doubting there's anyone out there for me isn't helping."*
Inside Eyebrow:	*"No, that's not helping."*
Outside Eyebrow:	*"Not helping at all."*
Under Eye:	*"That's not helping."*
Nose:	*"I need to change that."*
Chin:	*"What if there IS someone out there for me?"*
Collarbone:	*"I'd be okay with that."*
Under Arm:	*"I'd really be okay with that."*
Head:	*"I choose to believe there is someone out there for me."*
Inside Eyebrow:	*"There is someone out there for me."*
Outside Eyebrow:	*"There is someone out there for me."*
Under Eye:	*"I feel better just thinking that…"*
Nose:	*"I feel kind of excited…"* (Sighs)
Chin:	*"And happy…"*
Collarbone:	*"Thinking this."*
Under Arm:	*"I choose to believe there is someone out there for me."*

It's time to check in with Julie and see how intense the original fear still is for her. I have her say the original statement aloud and with conviction:

"I am afraid that there's no one out there for me."

Her current intensity level has dropped to a four. When there is still *any* intensity, go back to the karate chop point and continue to tap with this modified tapping statement:

"Even though I still have a little fear that there's no one out there for me, I deeply love and accept myself."

"Even though I still have a little fear that there's no one out there for me, I deeply love and accept myself."

"Even though I still have a little fear that there's no one out there for me, I deeply love and accept myself."

Tap at least seven times on each of the tapping points using these tapping phrases:

Head:	*"This remaining fear…"*
Inside Eyebrow:	*"This remaining fear and doubt."* (Sighs)
Outside Eyebrow:	*"I am ready to release it…"*
Under Eye:	*"And embrace the possibility that there IS someone out there for me."*
Nose:	*"I like that idea much better."* (Sighs)
Chin:	*"I choose to entertain that possibility."*
Collarbone:	*"I choose to see that as a certainty…"*
Under Arm:	*"And not just a possibility."*
Head:	*"Yea for me!"*
Inside Eyebrow:	*"Yea for me!"*
Outside Eyebrow:	*"I accept and embrace the idea that…"* (Yawns)
Under Eye:	*"There is someone out there for me."*
Nose:	*"I relax into that idea."*
Chin:	*"I love this idea."*

Collarbone:	*"I don't know why I didn't accept it before..."*
	(Yawns)
Under Arm:	*"But I accept it now."*

Head:	*"I accept the idea...maybe even the fact..."*
Inside Eyebrow:	*"That there is someone out there for me."*
Outside Eyebrow:	*"There is someone out there for me..."*
Under Eye:	*"Even though I haven't met them yet."*
Nose:	*"I look forward to the day I meet them..."* (Yawns)
Chin:	*"I wonder if I'll recognize them..."*
Collarbone:	*"As my SoulMate..."*
Under Arm:	*"Or if it will take a while."*

Head:	*"I don't care really..."*
Inside Eyebrow:	*"I'm just happy to know they are out there."*
Outside Eyebrow:	*"I'm happy to know I have someone..."*
Under Eye:	*"Who wants to be with me..."*
Nose:	*"As much as I want to be with them."*
Chin:	*"Yipee!"*
Collarbone:	*"Hooray for me!"*
Under Arm:	*"There is someone out there for me!"*

Since Julie is now smiling widely, we stop and check in with her to see if there is any intensity left for the original fear. Again, I have her say that statement aloud and with conviction:

"I am afraid that there's no one out there for me."

She laughs when saying it. The intensity level is now at a two. So I ask, "What keeps it from being a zero?" She says, "I haven't met him yet." This is a new aspect; therefore we create a new tapping statement to clear that aspect:

"Even though I've not met my SoulMate yet, which makes me doubt he exists, I deeply love and accept myself."

She rates the intensity level for that doubt to be about a three. Going back to the karate chop point, she taps while repeating the tapping statement aloud and with conviction three times.

"Even though I've not met my SoulMate yet, which makes me doubt he exists, I deeply love and accept myself."

"Even though I've not met my SoulMate yet, which makes me doubt he exists, I deeply love and accept myself."

"Even though I've not met my SoulMate yet, which makes me doubt he exists, I deeply love and accept myself."

Then I have her tap at least seven times on each of the following tapping points while repeating aloud:

Head:	*"Since I haven't met my SoulMate yet…"*
Inside Eyebrow:	*"I doubt he exists."*
Outside Eyebrow:	*"I've never met the president of the United States either…"*
Under Eye:	*"So I doubt he exists."* (Huh?)
Nose:	*"There are lots of people I've never met…"*
Chin:	*"Do I doubt their existence?"*
Collarbone:	*"It's entirely possible that my SoulMate exists…"*
Under Arm:	*"and I just haven't met him yet."*
Head:	*"Oh, I get it!"* (Laughs)
Inside Eyebrow:	*"It's the same thing."*
Outside Eyebrow:	*"Duh!"*

Under Eye:	*"It's entirely possible that my SoulMate exists…"*
	(Yawns)
Nose:	*"And I just haven't met him yet."*
Chin:	*"Boy, will I feel silly when I do meet him."*
Collarbone:	*"I'll have to tell him I didn't believe he existed."*
Under Arm:	*"I'll bet he'll get a laugh out of that."*
Head:	*"I hope he'll get a laugh out of that."*
Inside Eyebrow:	*"That'll be funny."*
Outside Eyebrow:	*"Oh, silly me!"*
Under Eye:	*"This is one thing I don't mind being wrong about."*
Nose:	*"I love being wrong about this."*
Chin:	*"My SoulMate exists."*
Collarbone:	*"I just haven't met him yet."* (Sighs)
Under Arm:	*"And so it is."*

I stop Julie again and have her rate her intensity level for this statement:

"I am afraid that there's no one out there for me."

It is now a zero. As always, we test to see if she can make the intensity level come back up. I have her close her eyes and see if she can imagine anything that would make the intensity level increase. She can't think of anything. "It's like I don't know why I ever thought that. I mean, maybe I'm just impatient. I want to have children and I'm not getting any younger."

Installation of Desired Beliefs

For Julie, this is a complex issue with many aspects. Installing desired beliefs supports her ability to try new behaviors. We selected these beliefs to reinforce and install:

"I am open to meeting new people."

"I know there is someone out there for me."

"I believe my SoulMate exists."

When you tap several rounds on all the tapping points using these statements, you reinforce the truth of them. You install them. Soon you will notice that your belief in the statement is high and, even better yet, that the newly installed belief is manifesting good things in your life.

Outer Work: You Gotta Be Bad, You Gotta Be Bold, You Gotta Be Wiser

In this exercise you will create personalized tapping statements for yourself. Like a Chinese menu, combine one option from the first column with one from the second into a complete tapping statement using the following formula:

"Even though I am afraid of being _____ again,
_____."

Select one or two at the most	Select an ending to the tapping statement
Hurt	I deeply love and accept myself.
Used	
Abused	What if I'm not this time?
Vulnerable	

Select one or two at the most	Select an ending to the tapping statement
Rejected	I choose to live with an open heart.
Disappointed	
Smothered	What if I'm wiser now?
Abandoned	
Humiliated	What if I see the signs this time?
Naive	
Wrong	I choose to take manageable risks.
Shamed	
	I open to love anyhow.
INSERT FAVORITE "FEAR" HERE	

Here are examples:

"Even though I am afraid of being <u>Wrong</u> *again,* <u>What if I'm not this time?</u>*"*

and

"Even though I am afraid of being <u>Vulnerable</u> *again,* <u>I choose to live with an open heart.</u>*"*

Next rate the intensity level. Then start to tap as instructed in chapter 4. Feel free to adapt some of the tapping phrases from the examples throughout the book for your own use. Continue tapping until your intensity level reaches zero and, after testing, all additional aspects have been cleared.

One of my students reported changing one of her main fears about losing herself in a relationship. "I began with a nine intensity level on that one. Again the tapping worked. Later in the class I wrote, 'I understand that I am NOT going to lose myself in a relationship... I will choose a partner who would not want that for me either.' Then, in an exercise at the end of the course, I wrote, 'I can be comfortable with the notion of us being part of each other and yet distinct individuals. Instead of fearing losing myself, I feel opportunities for personal growth together and for increased joy.'"

What's Next?

In chapter 8 you will learn to use EFT to promote self-love and self-nurturing. Most of my clients have some degree of difficulty with self-love. Women especially confuse self-love and self-nurturing with selfishness because our traditional role is that of caretaker for others. This curtails the speed at which your SoulMate manifests. The old saying about having to love yourself before someone else can love you is true. SoulMate relationships are the pairing of abundant equals, not two halves trying to get love from each other so that they can feel whole.

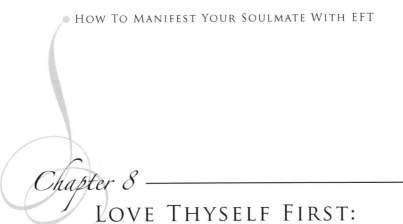

Chapter 8
Love Thyself First:
Self-Love and Nurturance

"To love oneself is the beginning of a life-long romance."

Oscar Wilde

DO YOU LIKE spending time alone? Are you your own worst critic? Are you a perfectionist? Do you apologize frequently? Break promises to yourself? Are you a people pleaser? Do you have difficulties saying no to even simple requests? Do you get enough rest and exercise? Are you caught up in an addiction to a substance, process or person? Is it hard for you to accept a compliment with a simple thank you?

Difficulties with self-love are common in Western cultures. When he was younger, the Dalai Lama was baffled by the trouble Westerners have with self-esteem. He went around a group of Westerners and asked, "Do you have that [trouble]?" When most people said yes, he responded, "Oh, very strange, self-esteem."

In my years of clinical practice, low self-esteem and lack of self-love is the common denominator among clients. In fact, I've come to think of it as part of the reason they are troubled and need my help. I am startled by how resistant people are to doing anything nice or nurturing for themselves, especially women. They fear being selfish. This intense clinging to a martyr role doesn't serve anyone. It makes you brittle, not resilient. It contributes to all kinds of unhappiness and relationship troubles.

Self-love is meant to be your foundation. It is your birthright. Once you get it – once you really feel what it is like to love yourself… to fall in love with yourself – you might never want to leave this stage. You'll want the romance to last forever. It can – once you recognize that it is not selfish, narcissistic or self-absorbed. As author Byron Katie says, "Just keep coming home to yourself. You are the one you've been waiting for."

When you truly love yourself, you *are* enough. Your happiness and well-being become a top priority. You don't let anyone treat you badly because you know that you deserve the best love life has to offer. You take excellent care of yourself – mentally, emotionally, physically and spiritually. Deep in your soul you know that you are worthy just because you are here, just because you exist. You delight in yourself. You are fascinated by your life, your thoughts, your body and your feelings. You are gentle and compassionate with yourself. You are kind and patient with yourself and others. You do nice things for yourself – including occasional treats. You may even hug yourself. You are filled with gratitude.

In short, you think, feel and act towards yourself exactly the way you would towards a lover, and in the same way you would want them to treat you. In this way you show others how to treat you and what you deserve. By giving to yourself you are fulfilled, abundant and generous. You have spare love to share. As personal development expert Shakti Gawain says, "My willingness to be intimate with my own deep feelings created the space for intimacy with another." It is for this reason that self-love is not selfish.

Self-love diminishes no one. It blesses others. It's yummy to love yourself. It feels good. When you truly love yourself, you are radiant, charismatic and irresistible to your SoulMate.

If you are depleted, lacking in self-love and need someone to come along to fill you up with love – to "give" you love – you will attract someone who will either manipulate you, take advantage of you or mirror your lack of fullness right back to you. We *always* attract partners who confirm how we think, feel and behave towards ourselves. If you believe that nobody can love you, you will attract emotionally unavailable, neglectful or abusive partners. If you believe you aren't attractive, your partners will be critical of your appearance in just the way you are towards yourself. In short, if you are not excited about yourself and your life, or are attracting less-than-desirable partners, you've got some work to do to increase your self-love.

What I most enjoy about dating is what I call the "Me too!" phase. This is the delicious time, usually early in a relationship, when you discover all the things you two have in common that you thought no one else shared. It makes you feel validated, connected and less alone. The thought that goes along with it is "He is like me. I like him when he is like me."

How does this connect to self-love? Think about it; if you fall in love with people who are like you in important ways, what you are really saying is that you love yourself; you love the things about the other person that you love about yourself. In short, you are falling in love with yourself all over again by connecting with others who are like yourself.

However, there is the inevitable "Oh no!" phase when you discover that the person you are infatuated with is not like you. They are different in ways you didn't expect or foresee. This is when self-love is particularly important, because when you love yourself you are not threatened by the other person's differences. In fact, you celebrate them and think, "Isn't that *interesting* about him!" This is when SoulMate love really starts. The "Me too!" phase is when our egos connect. It is the ability to love the other person for differences – for their otherness – that is the beginning of SoulMate love.

When you can celebrate and share each other's differences, you evolve together. Your heart and your ability to love expand to take in their differences and relate to them as an "other," not just another version of yourself.

Here's a story from one of my SoulMate ManiFest students:

"I stayed in bed doing EFT for over an hour this morning. Worked on clearing icky words, thoughts, abandonment issues and how they related to my being able to give love freely and without fear. Kept forgetting to do the zero to ten scale before starting, but my upset level must have been high to start because with each phrase I began to cry almost immediately.

"It's funny... it's as if the neural pathways to the previous anger and hurt have been filled in. I no longer go there automatically. Good! I am happy to have had some realizations: that it was me allowing (on some level) the hurtful words from Mom to hold me back; that I can now choose to see myself differently... as a brave woman who chooses to take risks in life (risking to meet new people, new men... risking to try love again).

"What was once true for me is true no longer. Now I trust myself to say no to whatever is not right for me. I trust myself to be friendly, interested and interesting. I trust that when my SoulMate and I meet we will have a "knowing" and that our relationship will flow with grace and ease, because I am doing the work from my side to release old thoughts and patterns that no longer serve me. I am now willing to let down the barriers to love, once installed for my own protection to keep me from moving into relationships before I'd done my work. I am loving myself and am able to say, 'no thanks, not right for me' easily and efficiently."

Your Fairy Godmother Says, *"Simply Irresistible!"*

"Self-love is where it's at. Stand in self-love and let the world come to you. Don't seek the approval of others at the expense of yourself. Seek your own approval first and foremost. The opposite of self-love isn't self-hate; it's self-denial. When you love yourself you are generous with yourself.

"Self-love is waking up to the wonder of your own life. I hope you realize you are amazing. If you could see yourself the way I see you, you would never doubt it. You take my breath away! I am so proud of you. Those who can't see this about you are blinded by their own lack of self-love.

"People who love themselves like you do (or will soon) love others easily and abundantly. There is a generosity to their caring. This is very attractive. People who love themselves are a tribe who recognize and appreciate each other. People who love themselves are humble and matter-of-fact. They feel no need to brag or prove what is obvious.

"Don't go looking for love in all the wrong places. Go looking for love in the first place – inside yourself. Being loved by another is just a reflection of what you love about yourself. You can never lose the love that starts from within. So if you are looking for love, start looking inside your own heart – not begging with your hand out. You don't *find* love, you source it from within. You *become* love. Cultivate that and you will be in love forever.

"Psst... those critical, blaming or belittling voices inside your head are liars. You are perfect – not because you are skinny, rich or pleasing to be around; self-love is unconditional. You are lovable because you are you-nique! Start treating and thinking of yourself that way."

Inner Work: I Will Survive!

In the following tapping sequence you will learn how to clear significant barriers to self-love. Even though you might not be able to relate to Chuck's issue, you are encouraged to borrow benefits by tapping along with the following sequence. Please note that if this topic triggers intense feelings for you because of your own abuse, contact a trained professional for support and assistance.

Chuck is 42 years old, divorced and living alone. Because he was sexually abused in his youth by a teen minister, he drinks a little more than he should. He has persistent feelings of shame and disgust that are directed at himself – a sign of lack of self-love and self-forgiveness.

For this session, we start with the tapping statement:

> *"Even though I feel ashamed and disgusted with myself because of what happened to me, I deeply love and forgive myself."*

His intensity level in the present for this statement is a 20 (on a scale of zero = no distress whatsoever and 10 = the most intense distress you can imagine)! It's pretty bad for him. I am glad that at this point we have a good rapport built up and a history of successfully reducing the emotional intensity of other issues. This gives Chuck the confidence to move into a scary issue.

Begin by tapping on the karate chop point, repeating the entire tapping statement three times aloud and with conviction:

> *"Even though I feel ashamed and disgusted with myself because of what happened to me, I deeply love and forgive myself."*

> *"Even though I feel ashamed and disgusted with myself because of what happened to me, I deeply love and forgive myself."*

> *"Even though I feel ashamed and disgusted with myself because of what happened to me, I deeply love and forgive myself."*

Tap at least seven times on each of the following tapping points while repeating aloud the tapping phrases below....

Head:	*"This shame and disgust..."*
Inside Eyebrow:	*"Shame and disgust..."* (Sighs)
Outside Eyebrow:	*"My feelings of shame and disgust..."*
Under Eye:	*"These feelings of shame and disgust..."*
Nose:	*"That have haunted me all my life..."*
Chin:	*"I can't drink them away...."*
Collarbone:	*"I try to drink them away..."*
Under Arm:	*"But they only come back when I sober up."*

Head:	*"These thoughts and feelings about myself..."*
Inside Eyebrow:	*"That I can never be rid of..."*
Outside Eyebrow:	*"They are ruining my life."*
Under Eye:	*"Ruining my life."*
Nose:	*"Shame and disgust are ruining my life..."* (Sighs)
Chin:	*"Ruining and running my life."*
Collarbone:	*"Shame and disgust are ruining and running my life."*
Under Arm:	*"And I can't escape them... or drown them."*

Head:	*"What if I forgive myself?"*
Inside Eyebrow:	*"Forgive myself..."*
Outside Eyebrow:	*"Forgive myself for what happened to me."*
Under Eye:	*"For being a kid..."*
Nose:	*"For trusting an adult..."*
Chin:	*"Who was supposed to be a good person."*
Collarbone:	*"My fault was trusting an adult..."*
Under Arm:	*"Who was supposed to be a good person."*

Head:	*"How was a kid supposed to know that he wasn't a good person?"*

Inside Eyebrow:	*"He was my dad's friend."*
Outside Eyebrow:	*"He should have been safe…"*
Under Eye:	*"He was a man of the church."*
Nose:	*"I trusted him."*
Chin:	*"I was supposed to be able to trust him."*
Collarbone:	*"I was supposed to be able to trust him."*
Under Arm:	*"But he hurt me instead."*

Head:	*"He hurt me and I couldn't tell anybody."*
Inside Eyebrow:	*"He hurt me and I couldn't tell anybody."*
Outside Eyebrow:	*"He hurt me and I never told anybody."*
Under Eye:	*"I felt so dirty and disgusted."*
Nose:	*"I thought I did something to make this happen."*
Chin:	*"I must be bad…"*
Collarbone:	*"I must be dirty and disgusting…"*
Under Arm:	*"To have something like that happen to me."*

Head:	*"I hate that this happened to me."*
Inside Eyebrow:	*"I hate how bad it made me feel…"*
Outside Eyebrow:	*"About myself…"* (Sighs)
Under Eye:	*"About him…"*
Nose:	*"About the church…"*
Chin:	*"About my dad…"* (Yawns)
Collarbone:	*"About life!"*
Under Arm:	*"I wish this never would have happened!"*

Head:	*"I wish this never would have happened!"*
Inside Eyebrow:	*"Because it made me hate myself."*
Outside Eyebrow:	*"I hate myself…"*
Under Eye:	*"And I really want to love myself…"*
Nose:	*"Love and protect myself…"*
Chin:	*"I'm worth loving and protecting…"*

Collarbone:	*"Even though I don't fully recognize it yet…"*
Under Arm:	*"I'm worth loving and protecting…"*

Head:	*"Even though my dad couldn't protect me…"*
Inside Eyebrow:	*"He didn't know…"*
Outside Eyebrow:	*"It was too disgusting to tell him…"*
Under Eye:	*"Besides, what if he didn't believe me?"*
Nose:	*"It was his friend after all."*
Chin:	*"I was too afraid to tell…"*
Collarbone:	*"And have my dad not believe me…"*
Under Arm:	*"Or worse… to blame me."* (Sobs)

Head:	*"I kept quiet to protect myself…"*
Inside Eyebrow:	*"And to protect my dad."*
Outside Eyebrow:	*"I didn't want to lose his love…"*
Under Eye:	*"It's all I had…"*
Nose:	*"It's all I had because…"*
Chin:	*"I hated myself…"*
Collarbone:	*"When I wanted to love myself."*
Under Arm:	*"I still want to love myself."*

Head:	*"I want to love myself…"*
Inside Eyebrow:	*"But I'm afraid it's too late."*
Outside Eyebrow:	*"I still feel disgusted…"*
Under Eye:	*"Because of what someone else did to me."*
Nose:	*"That man put his self-hate and self-disgust on me…"*
Chin:	*"And, good boy that I am, I adopted it."*
Collarbone:	*"I carried it for him…"*
Under Arm:	*"I carried it for him…"*

Head:	*"Maybe I've carried it long enough."*
Inside Eyebrow:	*"I've carried it long enough."*

Outside Eyebrow:	*"It's time I gave it back to him…"*
Under Eye:	*"Time to recognize it was not about me…"*
Nose:	*"But about him trying to get rid of his self-hate and disgust…"*
Chin:	*"By giving it to me."*
Collarbone:	*"He gave it to me…"*
Under Arm:	*"Now I'm giving it back."*
Head:	*"I'm giving it back…"*
Inside Eyebrow:	*"Since it wasn't mine in the first place."*
Outside Eyebrow:	*"What was and is mine is self-love and forgiveness…"*
Under Eye:	*"Even though I'm not yet sure I deserve it."*
Nose:	*"I can learn to deserve it…"*
Chin:	*"I've always wanted to love and forgive myself…"*
Collarbone:	*"I choose to love and forgive myself…"*
Under Arm:	*"Even though it feels foreign right now…"*
Head:	*"I choose to love and forgive myself…"*
Inside Eyebrow:	*"Even though it feels foreign right now…"* (Yawns)
Outside Eyebrow:	*"It'll get better with time…"*
Under Eye:	*"And practice."*
Nose:	*"Even though I can't imagine this changing…"*
Chin:	*"I am willing to begin the process…"*
Collarbone:	*"Begin loving and forgiving myself…"*
Under Arm:	*"For being wrong all these years…"*
Head:	*"For thinking this was MY shame and disgusting act…"*
Inside Eyebrow:	*"When it was really HIS!"*
Outside Eyebrow:	*"I don't mind being wrong about that."*
Under Eye:	*"I love being wrong about that."*
Nose:	*"I can still learn to love and forgive myself…"*

Chin:	*"For being a good boy…"*
Collarbone:	*"A trusting boy…"*
Under Arm:	*"Who protected his father…"*

It's time to check in with Chuck. His intensity level started at a 20. He's now down to a six. We decide to continue tapping with this modified tapping statement, which he repeats aloud and with conviction three times while tapping on the karate chop point:

"Even though I STILL feel ashamed and disgusted with myself because of what happened to me, I deeply love and forgive myself."

"Even though I STILL feel ashamed and disgusted with myself because of what happened to me, I deeply love and forgive myself."

"Even though I STILL feel ashamed and disgusted with myself because of what happened to me, I deeply love and forgive myself."

Go back to the tapping points….

Head:	*"This remaining shame and disgust…"*
Inside Eyebrow:	*"Remaining shame and disgust"*
Outside Eyebrow:	*"I am already releasing it…"*
Under Eye:	*"And embracing self-love and forgiveness."*
Nose:	*"Releasing shame and disgust…"*
Chin:	*"Embracing self-love and forgiveness."*
Collarbone:	*"Even though it doesn't feel normal…"*
Under Arm:	*"I look forward to the day that it does."* (Nodding)

Head:	*"Today I take the first step to loving and forgiving myself."*
Inside Eyebrow:	*"One step closer…"*
Outside Eyebrow:	*"One step closer…"*

Under Eye:	*"It will feel normal one day…"*
Nose:	*"I will feel normal one day…"*
Chin:	*"Even though I don't believe it right now."*
Collarbone:	*"I take the first step to love and forgive myself."* (Sighs)
Under Arm:	*"All I have to do right now is begin."*

Head:	*"When I love and forgive myself…"*
Inside Eyebrow:	*"I will see things rightly."*
Outside Eyebrow:	*"I've been confused all these years…"*
Under Eye:	*"Now I choose to put that right."*
Nose:	*"I have been confused about my own worth…"*
Chin:	*"And I choose to understand…"*
Collarbone:	*"And embrace the lovability…"*
Under Arm:	*"I always craved."*

Head:	*"What if I am lovable?"*
Inside Eyebrow:	*"What if I am innocent of wrongdoing?"*
Outside Eyebrow:	*"What if it wasn't my 'sin'?"*
Under Eye:	*"I am innocent…"*
Nose:	*"Innocent like a child…"*
Chin:	*"A lovable, innocent child…"*
Collarbone:	*"The lovable and innocent child…"*
Under Arm:	*"Who was taken from me."*

Head:	*"I embrace that child inside of me…"*
Inside Eyebrow:	*"And love him for surviving…"*
Outside Eyebrow:	*"I love his innocence…"*
Under Eye:	*"I love his trusting nature…"*
Nose:	*"I love his desire to protect his father…"*
Chin:	*"At his own expense."*
Collarbone:	*"Brave, unselfish boy…"*
Under Arm:	*"Brave, unselfish boy."*

It's time to check in and see how intense the original tapping statement feels for Chuck right now.

"I feel ashamed and disgusted with myself because of what happened to me."

Intensity level = three. The intensity level is still dropping, but not to zero yet. I ask Chuck, "What keeps it at a three?" He replies, "I've hurt so many people because of this through my drinking… my ex-wife… my daughters… myself."

This is a new aspect. Therefore we create a new tapping statement and determine its intensity level:

"Even though I've hurt so many people because of my drinking, I deeply love and forgive myself."

Chuck rates the intensity level for this statement at a seven. Because Chuck is now an experienced tapper, we elect to have him tap by himself on this new aspect and any others that arise. When I see him next, he reports that the intensity level for the original statement is now at a zero.

Chuck's comments: "I figured I was using the drinking to deal with the feelings of shame and disgust, but I didn't think until we tapped last time that I was hurting anybody but myself. But when you got me thinking about that brave, unselfish little boy who was protecting his dad by not ratting out his dad's friend, it occurred to me that I was hurting him."

Now that the intensity is at a zero for the original tapping statement, we test to see if Chuck can make the intensity level go back up. He closes his eyes and repeats the original tapping statement silently to himself to notice what happens. When he opens his eyes, he says, "It's funny. I see it completely differently now. I am no longer ashamed and disgusted with myself. I'm disgusted at what happened to me, but not at myself. I'm angry that this happened to me and that I let it affect my life for so long, but I'm glad it's over now."

Note: There may be additional aspects for Chuck to work on around this issue, but this is a great start!

Installation of Desired Beliefs

For Chuck, since this is such an intense and chronic issue, installing desired beliefs is critical. Often those who are abused as children form a *victim identity*. We selected these beliefs to reinforce and install:

"I am a survivor."

"I am a brave and unselfish person."

"I love the child I was and the man I am now."

These are only a few of the affirming statements that Chuck (or you) might need. It's a good start. Tap several rounds on each of these statements to install them.

Outer Work: Gimmee Gimmee Good Lovin'

In this exercise you will create personalized tapping statements for yourself. Like a Chinese menu, combine one option from the first column with one from the second into a complete tapping statement using the following formula:

"Even though I don't love myself because _____,
_____."

Select one	Select an ending for the tapping statement
Something bad happened to me	I deeply love and forgive myself anyway.
I'm not perfect	
No one ever really loved me	What if it doesn't matter and I'm loveable anyhow?
I drink/do drugs	
I'm overweight	What if I'm lovable just the way I am?
I don't make a lot of money	
I am too selfish	I choose to love myself anyway.
I made mistakes	
I am insecure	I forgive and love myself right now.
I don't deserve love	
I am not lovable	
My parents didn't want me	
INSERT FAVORITE "FLAW" HERE	

Here are examples:

> *"Even though I don't love myself because* <u>My parents didn't want me,</u> <u>What</u> <u>if it doesn't matter and I'm loveable anyhow?"</u>

and

> *"Even though I don't love myself because* <u>I made mistakes,</u> <u>I choose to love</u> <u>myself anyway."</u>

Next rate the intensity level. Then start to tap as instructed in chapter 4. Feel free to adapt some of the tapping phrases from the examples throughout the book for your own use. Continue tapping until your intensity level reaches zero and, after testing, all additional aspects have been cleared.

Bonus #2: Just Because I Love You! Fat-Bottomed Girls You Make the Rockin' World Go Round

> *"Even though I am too* _____ *to manifest my*
> *SoulMate,_____."*

Select one or two at the most	Select an ending to the tapping statement
Old	I deeply love and accept myself.
Fat	What if I'm not?
Poor	What if it is possible anyway?
Scared	

Select one or two at the most	Select an ending to the tapping statement
Skeptical	What if my SoulMate LOVES that about me?
Damaged	
Depressed	I choose to see my _____ in a positive light.
Short	
Ugly	I choose to love this about myself.
Naïve	
Rigid	I choose to do so anyway.
Set in my ways	
Busy	What if I'm just right?
Brokenhearted	
Flawed	I deeply love and forgive myself.
Much of a dreamer	
Closed off	I am open to love anyhow.
INSERT FAVORITE "FLAW" HERE	

Here are examples:

> *"Even though I am afraid I am too <u>Damaged</u> to manifest my SoulMate, <u>What if my SoulMate LOVES that about me?</u>"*

and

> *"Even though I am afraid I am too <u>Much of a dreamer</u> to manifest my SoulMate, <u>What if it is possible anyway?</u>"*

Next rate the intensity level. Then start to tap as instructed in chapter 4. Feel free to adapt some of the tapping phrases from the examples throughout the book for your own use. Continue tapping until your intensity level reaches zero and, after testing, all additional aspects have been cleared.

What's Next?

In chapter 9 you will learn how to use EFT to be more open and allowing of love. Couples therapists Gay and Kathlyn Hendricks say you have an upper limit to the amount of love, joy and good feeling you allow into your life. These limits are set by what you think you deserve. Ready to get rid of those limits and allow love into your life?

Chapter 9
ALLOW FOR LOVE:
BE RECEPTIVE AND GIVING

"The more we seek love, the more it eludes us. ...And when we give up our attachment to the outcome of our loving, then real Love can flow. The more we consciously choose to extend Love, the more Love we have."

HENRY GRAYSON

ALLOWING REQUIRES INNER WORK and outer work to keep your heart open, lest you succumb to what author Jeff Brown cautions about: "Closing the heart is a self-fulfilling prophecy." To allow someone to come into your heart-house, you have to open the door. Most doors open from the inside. To manifest your SoulMate you have to either invite others into your world or go out into their world. Either way, you have to open the door.

Allowing for love is how you become an abundant fountain of love – sharing with *everyone* – not a deep, dry well wanting to be filled up by *someone*. Even if you haven't received a lot of love from others in your life *yet* doesn't mean you lack love or that you will never share love with another. Love is the essence of your soul. The trick is to discover and turn on the tap now. Let love flow out of you in big and small acts of kindness. Love is kindness with its work clothes on.

Loving people are magnetic. To attract your SoulMate, BE the loving person you want to be, and do it NOW. Don't wait for your SoulMate to appear in order to turn on the tap. That's backwards. Without practice, it might not work when you want and need it the most. Love is like a muscle that gets stronger with practice.

Don't be miserly with love. Don't save it up or keep it until that special someone comes along. The practice of giving and receiving love is necessary throughout life. Everyone needs love, so be generous with your love. What are you saving it for? Enjoy the flow of love through you. Pour it out into the world. It's joyful and awesome. It's magical... and it will attract your SoulMate. Remember that what you give out always returns to you in some form.

I feel sad when my clients say that they withhold expressions of love because of fears, or because they are waiting for the other person to say it first or give to them before they open up. In my clinical practice, I often see the results of such fear and withholding in crumbling marriages. A woman says that she doesn't fully open herself to give and receive love because she knows that he will just leave. Guess what? Because her partner is not getting all the love she has to give, he goes looking for it elsewhere. This confirms and manifests what she believes. Her beliefs help bring it about by restricting her behavior.

Yes, if you want to receive love, you have to give it. You first! Don't wait for someone else to show and share love first. Just start and see where it goes. By giving love to others you are placing yourself in the endless flow of love you desire. You become the source and force of love.

By the way, when talking about giving love first, I don't mean giving sex. Giving sex to get love doesn't work. Sex is an expression of love, not a prerequisite. It is shared openly and naturally when it is mutually desired and valued by both people. Then it is given as a gift to each other. SoulMates know sex is sacred and treat it like a sacrament.

Fear is what shuts down the flow of your love out into the world. Sometimes when I don't know what to do in a situation, I ask myself, "What would love do?" Love is always the answer. Marianne Williamson says that every action is either an expression of love or a cry for love. Look at your actions. What do they express?

Loving is about allowing this flow of inner abundance to go out into the world. Allowing is about getting your ego out of the way – removing the fears, the "should haves," the rules, the self-doubts and the limiting beliefs. Allow loving thoughts to fill your mind. Allow loving actions to fill your day. Allow loving feelings to fill your heart. Allow a loving spirit to fill your soul.

Perceive and Receive

You cannot *make* someone love you, but you can *allow* it. Allow yourself to perceive and receive loving actions from others. Sometimes this is the scariest part because you fear being indebted to someone when you accept acts of kindness. Or you might think that this means something that isn't intended by the sender, such as "You are weak if you need things from others." Phhhh!

When you are blocked from receiving love, your SoulMate could pass you by. Common fears and beliefs that block others from giving love to you include:

- I don't need other people.

- People are only in it for themselves.

- Letting others give to me is a sign of weakness.

- I'm going to be manipulated if I accept caring from others.

- I can't trust their intentions.

- It's selfish to receive.

Some of these may sound silly to you as you read them. Consider the possibility that there are ways you have not been open to the love that someone wanted to give you because of some belief or fear about receiving.

There is nothing virtuous about giving exclusively, especially in a relationship. If you are only the giver, then your relationship will be one-sided; there will be no energetic interplay that energizes you as a couple. The initial compulsion to be only the giver is really about old roles you adopted early in life to try to win love. If you do this in your adult relationship, it will turn stale. A dynamic, lively, loving relationship involves taking turns giving and receiving love. Otherwise it becomes an ego-mate relationship – just playing out old roles and rules.

Maybe you don't know what loving actions look like, especially because we often use TV and movies as our reference points. Not everyone is going to whisk you off in a private jet to dinner and the opera in San Francisco or stand outside your window like John Cusack in *Say Anything* with a boombox over his head playing "In Your Eyes."

Maybe you grew up in an alcoholic or abusive family situation and you have been conditioned to believe that love comes hand in hand with abuse, criticism or neglect. This traumatic bonding seems normal to you. Until you break this conditioning, you will attract partners who will treat you in similar ways and call it love. It is not love. Or perhaps you run from partners who truly love you because it threatens old beliefs you hold about yourself, even though those beliefs are painful.

Gary Chapman, author of *The Five Love Languages*, tells us how love is demonstrated in ordinary ways through:

- **Words of affirmation**

- **Acts of service**

- **Thoughtful gifts**

- **Quality time spent together**

- **Physical affection**

Use these as guidelines. Determine your favorite ways to give and receive love. Communicate them to your beloved.

YOUR FAIRY GODMOTHER SAYS,

"Can't Keep It In, I Gotta Let It Out"

"Hallelujah! This is the best part. The doors open and the flow of love sweeps through. It is also the scariest part. Why is that? It is because the flow of love through your life initiates an alchemical transformation. Love changes you, grows you, and reveals all the places where your heart is small. SoulMate love is transformative. Not everyone is ready for that.

"If you don't want love to sweep into your life, the easiest way to block it is to live a fear-based life. What fun is that, right? Take risks. Challenge beliefs. Replace them with consciously chosen life- and love-affirming beliefs. Open to the mystery, for that is what love is — mysterious, unpredictable and therefore ultimately uncontrollable.

"It requires courage to love, courage to live, and courage to *be*. Allowing for love is a radical act of saying yes to all of life. You can say you want love, but when it comes in a form you don't understand or can't control, will you shrink from it and push it away?

"Real love is an expression of the best of you and others. It's moving, profound and essentially very simple at the same time.

"I could go on, but I want you to get to the exercises that follow so you don't have to stay a moment longer behind any of those walls you've built over the years."

Inner Work: I Want a Man to Keep Me Warm

Julie, our ambitious, driven attorney from chapter 5, has too much of what marriage and family therapist Dr. Pat Allen calls *masculine energy*. Her friends describe her as driven, successful, intelligent and goal-oriented. She approaches dating in the same way. She is searching to find love and achieve her goal of having a child in the next three years. Successful in every other endeavor in her life, she is puzzled as to why she's not being successful in finding her SoulMate. She is accustomed to *doing* rather than *being* in her feminine, open and receptive mode. She tends to take charge during a date, making most of the decisions about what they do and where they go.

She admits to being afraid to let others take charge for fear she wouldn't enjoy herself. She assumes that her dates aren't as capable as she is, or that they would ultimately try to control her life (like her father). This is in contrast to her deep desire to have less responsibility and someone to share the load with her.

After some discussion we decide to start by tapping on the following issue:

"I am afraid to let go and let a man take care of me."

Her intensity level for this fear is eight. She is *not* used to or comfortable with letting men take care of her. We begin by tapping on the karate chop point while she repeats aloud and with conviction:

"Even though I am used to and capable of being in charge, I comfortably allow a man to take care of me."

"Even though I am used to and capable of being in charge, I comfortably allow a man to take care of me."

"Even though I am used to and capable of being in charge, I comfortably allow a man to take care of me."

Go to the tapping points. Tap at least seven times on each point while repeating the following tapping phrases:

Head:	*"I need to be in charge."*
Inside Eyebrow:	*"I'm capable of taking care of myself."*
Outside Eyebrow:	*"I'm an independent woman."*
Under Eye:	*"What's wrong with that?"*
Nose:	*"I get tired of being independent…"* (Sighs)
Chin:	*"Making all the decisions…"*
Collarbone:	*"Always striving…"*
Under Arm:	*"No place to rest."*

Head:	*"It'd be nice to rest once in a while…"*
Inside Eyebrow:	*"Let somebody else take charge…"*
Outside Eyebrow:	*"Make the plans…"*
Under Eye:	*"Share the decisions…"*
Nose:	*"Take care of me a little bit."*
Chin:	*"I'd be okay with that."* (Yawns)
Collarbone:	*"No, I wouldn't."*
Under Arm:	*"Yes, I would."*

Head:	*"Maybe I could learn to be comfortable…"*
Inside Eyebrow:	*"Letting a man take charge…"*
Outside Eyebrow:	*"Letting a man take charge."*
Under Eye:	*"That'd be a relief."*
Nose:	*"Nothing permanent…"*
Chin:	*"More like taking turns…"*
Collarbone:	*"When one of us wants or needs…"*
Under Arm:	*"A break, nurturing or a rest."*

Head:	*"I could take turns."*
Inside Eyebrow:	*"I could take turns."* (Sighs)

Outside Eyebrow:	*"That might be fun."*
Under Eye:	*"That might be a lot of fun."*
Nose:	*"To be on the receiving end…"*
Chin:	*"For a change…"*
Collarbone:	*"Give when I want to or need to…"*
Under Arm:	*"And not have to give all the time."* (Sighs)

Head:	*"Even though I'm highly capable…"*
Inside Eyebrow:	*"I choose to allow a man…"*
Outside Eyebrow:	*"To be capable, too."*
Under Eye:	*"Men are capable…"*
Nose:	*"Just as capable…"*
Chin:	*"Or maybe more so…"*
Collarbone:	*"Than I am."*
Under Arm:	*"I choose to allow his light to shine."*

Head:	*"By taking charge all the time…"*
Inside Eyebrow:	*"Maybe I'm stifling his need to give…"*
Outside Eyebrow:	*"And that's why I'm not finding my SoulMate…"*
Under Eye:	*"Because I don't know how to receive."*
Nose:	*"Yet."*
Chin:	*"I know I can learn this…"*
Collarbone:	*"Because I've learned harder things."*
Under Arm:	*"I choose now to receive and let the man take charge."*

It's time to check in with Julie and see how intense this fear still is for her. I have her say the original statement aloud and with conviction:

"I am afraid to let go and let a man take care of me."

Her current intensity level has dropped to a four. She says, "I'm afraid men will try to dictate my life to me." In this round of tapping we include this additional aspect using the tapping statement below. Julie repeats this aloud and with conviction three times while tapping on the karate chop point:

"Even though I'm afraid of having my life dictated by a man, I deeply love and accept myself."

"Even though I'm afraid of having my life dictated by a man, I deeply love and accept myself."

"Even though I'm afraid of having my life dictated by a man, I deeply love and accept myself."

Go back to the tapping points. Tap at least seven times on each point while repeating the following tapping phrases:

Head:	*"I am afraid of having my life dictated by a man."*
Inside Eyebrow:	*"I am really afraid of being controlled by another man…"*
Outside Eyebrow:	*"Just like Dad controlled and dictated my life to me."*
Under Eye:	*"Just like I let Dad control me."*
Nose:	*"I thought that was how he showed me his love…"*
Chin:	*"But it was really about what he wanted…"*
Collarbone:	*"Not what I wanted."*
Under Arm:	*"I'm such a people pleaser!"* (Sighs)

Head:	*"Such a Daddy's girl."*
Inside Eyebrow:	*"Isn't it time I took charge of my own life?"*
Outside Eyebrow:	*"And planned my own course…"*
Under Eye:	*"Take charge of my love life…"*
Nose:	*"And pick who I want to date…"*
Chin:	*"And stop picking men Dad would approve of."*
Collarbone:	*"And stop trying to control them."* (Gasps)

Under Arm: *"I pick men that I can control…"*

Head: *"Because I am so afraid that they will try to control me."*

Inside Eyebrow: *"But I don't respect men I can control."*

Outside Eyebrow: *"They have no fire."*

Under Eye: *"I don't trust them to take care of me."* (Nodding)

Nose: *"I want a man who can't be controlled by me…"*

Chin: *"Who is strong enough to take charge…"*

Collarbone: *"And take care of me…"*

Under Arm: *"So I can relax and receive his caring."*

Head: *"I want to relax and not be controlled."*

Inside Eyebrow: *"I choose to be in charge of my own life."*

Outside Eyebrow: *"I also choose to share my life."*

Under Eye: *"Share my life… meaning…"*

Nose: *"Allowing myself to be influenced…"*

Chin: *"Not controlled."*

Collarbone: *"Influenced…"*

Under Arm: *"Not controlled."*

Head: *"There's a difference."*

Inside Eyebrow: *"A BIG difference."*

Outside Eyebrow: *"I know the difference…"*

Under Eye: *"And can choose what I allow in my life."*

Nose: *"I can relax…"*

Chin: *"And choose what I allow in my life."*

Collarbone: *"I can choose to take care of myself…"*

Under Arm: *"Or choose to allow someone else to give to me."*

Head: *"I have both options…"*

Inside Eyebrow: *"Always."*

Outside Eyebrow:	*"I always had both options…"*
Under Eye:	*"I'm just now recognizing it…"*
Nose:	*"And claiming both choices for myself."* (Yawns)
Chin:	*"Hurray for me!"*
Collarbone:	*"Hurray for choices."*
Under Arm:	*"Hurray for allowing others to love me."*

By the smile on her face, I know it's time to check in and see what, if any, intensity is left with the original statement:

"I am afraid to let go and let a man take care of me."

Julie reports that the intensity level now is at zero. Therefore it's time to test. Closing her eyes, as she is so familiar with doing by now, she tries to bring up any thought, feeling, memory or sensation that might drive the intensity level associated with the original statement back up. She cannot.

Installation of Desired Beliefs

To reinforce and fill the space that Julie's old fear occupied, we develop a few affirming beliefs to install now:

"I actively choose between allowing a man to take care of me and taking care of myself."

"I allow others to love me."

"I gratefully receive love from others.

I instruct her to do as many rounds of tapping on these positive beliefs as she feels will properly install them. These are only a few of the affirming statements that Julie (or you) might need. Go back to your SoulMate Love Story from chapter 2 to find some affirming beliefs you would like to install now. Tap several rounds on each of these statements to install them. Or better yet, read your SoulMate Love Story aloud one sentence at a time while tapping on all points. This will help install that story as a preview of coming attractions. In fact, tap yourself silly!

Outer Work: Don't Throw Our Love Away

In this exercise you will create personalized tapping statements for yourself. Like a Chinese menu, combine one option from the first column with one from the second into a complete tapping statement using the following formula:

"Even though I block love from flowing to me and through me by
_____, _____."

Select one	Select an ending to the tapping statement
Putting up walls	I deeply love and accept myself. (default)
Doubting someone's intention	
Fearing manipulation	I allow my SoulMate to come to me anyhow.
Testing them endlessly	
Picking users and losers	I am willing to change this.
Playing the martyr	

Select one	Select an ending to the tapping statement
Being stingy with my love	I am open to letting love in.
Numbing myself	
Isolating myself	
Not being honest	
Complaining	
Criticizing others	
Putting myself down	
INSERT FAVORITE "BLOCK" HERE	

Here are examples:

"Even though I block love from flowing to me and through me by <u>Isolating myself, I am willing to change this.</u>*"*

and

"Even though I block love from flowing to me and through me by <u>Doubting someone's intention, I am open to letting love in.</u>*"*

Next rate the intensity level. Then start to tap as instructed in chapter 4. Feel free to adapt some of the tapping phrases from the examples throughout the book for your own use. Continue tapping until your intensity level reaches zero and, after testing, all additional aspects have been cleared.

What's Next?

Chapter 10 shows you how to use EFT to release past attachments and become open to new possibilities. When you are tied to the past, there is no room for someone new to come into your life.

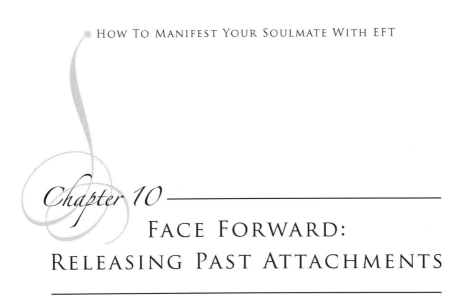

Chapter 10

FACE FORWARD:
RELEASING PAST ATTACHMENTS

"If you want the whole thing, the gods will give it to you. But you must be ready for it."

JOSEPH CAMPBELL

ALL STAGES OF manifesting are necessary and important, but this one of letting go and releasing past attachments seems to be the one people think they can skip. It's painful. Fortunately you now have EFT as a tool to release and move quickly through the painful parts.

Why is this necessary? You can't rise to a love in the future if you are carrying the weight of the past within you. Past attachments make you like a balloon tied to the ground; you're not free to soar, not free to manifest your SoulMate. Author Jeff Brown refers to the burden of past attachments as "the power of then." You can't go forward if you are looking backward.

What happens if you don't release past attachments? You will:

- **Repeat old patterns**

- Fail to integrate new learning

- Express grief in other relationships

- Form a victim identity

- Create/reinforce baggage

One of my clients did a releasing ritual in which she collected and burned some personal items leftover from her last relationship. In the presence of the other class members, she formed an intention to completely release that person (with love) and open herself to a new relationship. Within a month she met a new man and is still dating him over a year later. To her amazement he shares her love of art and theatre. At the time she listed these qualities on her SoulMate list, she thought she was never going to find someone like that.

Another client had been trying unsuccessfully to get closure with a former girlfriend he referred to as his "soulmate." By attempting to send her a package of stuff she'd left behind, he hoped to be done with her. Twice the package was returned as undeliverable. Instead of taking that as a message to fully and finally release her, he kept trying to contact her. Clearly he was still attached and not available for anyone new to come into his life. He reported a series of first dates that never turned into second dates. When he cleared that need to have one final form of contact with her by throwing away the package, he quickly started dating someone else.

Grief

First a word about releasing the past. No matter what you need to release, the process is always the same. It is one of self-forgiveness, grieving and letting go. Self-forgiveness is important because we've all made mistakes. You will continue to make mistakes as you move along this path. It is essential that you forgive yourself when you do.

The following overview is a brief discussion about the stages of grief as it applies to relationship attachments. Remember that grief comes in waves. It comes and goes. Each of the stages below can repeat and cycle back through your life at any time on the way to acceptance.

Stage One: Denial

This is the shocked and numb stage of grief. It protects you temporarily from the full blow of the loss. It is the "going through the motions" stage of grief. When feelings return, the "why me?" stage of anger is ushered in.

Loss happens to everyone. No one is exempt. After a romantic breakup, some people avoid the pain of grief by jumping quickly into a new relationship seeking the high of a new infatuation. By avoiding the pain and living in denial, they have not yet assimilated or benefitted from the lessons gained from the prior relationship, situation or change. These lessons are necessary to become the person who will manifest your SoulMate.

Stage Two: Anger

Anger, in this context, is your self-esteem reasserting itself. It is the part of you that was hurt and is in protest. I remember a time when I was walking a labyrinth that I helped build in my community. I was suffering over a recent break up. I was mad and thought it unfair. As I continued this walking meditation, I heard my thoughts protesting, "Why me? *I'm* not supposed to suffer." That thought stopped me in my tracks. I started laughing at myself because I thought I was exempt from the First Noble Truth in Buddhism, which is "Life is suffering." As long as I thought I should be exempt, I suffered. When I realized that I was attached to this belief, I could let it go. The anger ended.

Of course I suffer. All humans do. But when we are attached to the belief that we shouldn't have to – that we are special and an exemption should be made for us – we are stuck. If you are stuck in the angry phase of grief, you are attached to some belief about yourself, the other, or the way the world works. Take some time to pay attention to the thoughts that feed the anger. You can use EFT to change each one of these so that you are no longer mired in anger.

Release with love, not anger. That's the right vibration. If you are still angry, you're not done grieving. You are still attached.

Stage Three: Bargaining

Perhaps you fear letting go of your ex because you think you'll never find someone new. Or being Mr. or Mrs. X was your whole identity and you don't *yet* know who you are without that role. You might secretly harbor the hope that your ex will see the error of their ways, or they will realize that nobody will love them like you do and they will return to you. The bargaining stage of grief is when you ruminate about the "if onlys." Can you see how this preoccupation would prevent you from manifesting anyone new?

Stage Four: Depression

If your life seems empty and meaningless without your ex, then you are in the depressed stage of grief. You are in no position to start dating again. First of all, you won't have the energy. Nor will you have the desire. Second, if you allow yourself to descend like Persephone into the underworld of depression, expect to learn some important lessons. You will emerge with the spiritual wisdom of how to unite the dark and light within yourself. This alchemical process transforms you from a powerless victim to empowered and whole. An empowered, whole person is ready to manifest a SoulMate.

Stage Five: Acceptance

When you truly have accepted that a past relationship came into your life to teach you the *exact* lessons about yourself and about love that you need in order to manifest your SoulMate, you have finished grieving. You are truly at peace. This closure allows you to love and appreciate your ex for all they taught you and brought into your life. It allows you to move on. You are one step closer to manifesting your SoulMate.

There are four types of attachments to the past that need to be released:

- exes

- traumas

- outdated identities

- guilt

Release work is a grieving process in which you move from denial to acceptance. Completed grief work clears you emotionally and energetically, making you more fully available to manifest your SoulMate.

Releasing Exes

Releasing is not forgetting. It's honoring the love and lessons learned. Until you tuck your ex into the corner of your heart where exes belong, they occupy the center of your heart and block your ability to manifest your SoulMate. Your energy and thoughts are still preoccupied with them. If you try to send a clear signal to and call your SoulMate into your life, having unfinished business with your ex is like static on the line. The connection is frequently interrupted or your SoulMate can't take your call.

Releasing Trauma

Trauma is the result of a severely distressing event such as loss, injury, physical attack, sexual assault, life-threatening illness or a catastrophic event that taxes your ability to cope or make sense of the world. It is a psychological crisis.

When clients come to me who have unresolved trauma, they often say, "That's the past. I just want to put it behind me." They don't see the connection between what happened to them, the residual effects and their inability to manifest their SoulMate. It quickly becomes clear to me that they may have only scratched the surface of releasing the trauma. Those residual effects play out in their love lives. Unbeknownst to them they have unconsciously organized their lives to avoid similar situations and have become experts at numbing emotions through drinking, overeating, compulsive shopping or overworking themselves to the point of exhaustion. Unresolved trauma causes difficulties with trust, regulating emotions and setting and enforcing normal physical and emotional boundaries. All of these interfere with the creation of positive connections with others.

EFT is a powerful way to overcome the residual effects of trauma. However, please be advised that trauma work can require professional help and support.

Releasing Outdated Identities

You will manifest your SoulMate when you become the person they find irresistible. That requires a transformation of identity. You can't fake your way into an authentic, soul-deep relationship.

The following is a partial list of beliefs that represent outdated identities that can be blocking you from your SoulMate:

- **I am a victim/loser**

- I am independent

- I am a single person

- I'm not the marrying kind

Releasing an outdated identity is difficult because you are deeply invested in maintaining it, even if it keeps you stuck or miserable. Outdated identities include the blind spots you have about yourself. We all have them. We don't see ourselves objectively. Who would you have to become and what would you have to believe about yourself to attract exactly the SoulMate you desire?

One of my SoulMate ManiFest students reported, "Of all the possible fears about being in relationship, this was most relevant: That bad things had happened to me in the past (multiple failed marriages). I wondered if I was broken. I scored eleven out of ten as a starting intensity level on that one! It's been enough time now that *I can't remember the words I used to tap on...* guess they worked!" This experience of "forgetting" a previous problem is common with tapping.

Releasing Guilt

As Garrison Keillor said in his *Carnegie Hall Live* album, "Guilt is all that keeps some people in line." However, guilt does not help you move forward or manifest your SoulMate. Guilt is a case of the "shoulda, coulda, ough-tas." It makes us feel bad about ourselves, which is not very self-loving or in alignment with what you want to manifest.

Loving people are compassionate towards others. However, if that compassion doesn't start at home and doesn't include self-forgiveness, it is incomplete and lopsided. You can add self-forgiveness to any EFT tapping statement by inserting "I deeply love and *forgive* myself" instead of "I deeply love and *accept* myself."

YOUR FAIRY GODMOTHER SAYS,
"Release the Past to Allow the Future"

"You don't live in the past anymore, though a part of you thinks so. The past exists only in your mind. As long as you hang on to it, you will carry ghosts into the present and the future.

"You might think your past dooms or limits you. That is a mistake. Just because it's happened before doesn't mean it's going to happen again – unless you believe that. People get confused by that and hang on to that false belief to justify staying fearful and closed up.

"Who you were yesterday is not who you are today or will be tomorrow. There is a vast array of identities available to you. Why not pick one that will bring you everything your heart desires? Become fluid – become a shapeshifter.

"Trauma stories are no more valid or noble than stories of love and heroism. It's the attachment to the victim identity that causes you to lose touch with the amazing essence of who you really are. Trauma stories are like black holes in space. They suck up all the light available.

"Baggage is just the lies you tell yourself about the way things are. Those lies clutter up and obscure a clear perception of the world and other people. Learn to travel light. Do anything necessary to start each new relationship with a clean slate.

"Finally, guilt is a waste of time unless you learn how to be more loving the next time a similar situation presents itself. Use EFT to give yourself a guilt-ectomy!"

Inner Work: Please Release Me, Let Me Go

You might remember that Chuck had a significant relationship with Pamela that lasted four years. He assumed it was going to last forever, but she would never commit to him. About two years ago she broke it off to explore starting a second career. They remain friends. This mostly consists of his doing favors for her. Chuck dates occasionally, but always breaks up once the woman puts any demands on him, especially for more than friendship.

If you still have anger, hatred, jealousy, or sadness about your ex, you are still attached. If you secretly hope, like Chuck does, that your ex will see the light and want you back, you are still attached.

Chuck reluctantly agreed to this work. Obviously his hope of Pamela's return is high. So that is where we choose to start. "It's always best to start at the beginning," said Glinda to Dorothy as she was about to embark on the Yellow Brick Road to Oz.

The statement we choose to work with is:

"I don't want to give up the hope of Pamela's return."

Chuck's intensity level for this statement is a 10. We start by tapping on the karate chop point while repeating aloud and with conviction:

"Even though I don't want to give up the hope of Pamela's return, I deeply love and accept myself."

"Even though I don't want to give up the hope of Pamela's return, I deeply love and accept myself."

"Even though I don't want to give up the hope of Pamela's return, I deeply love and accept myself."

Tap along with Chuck to borrow the benefits. See what shifts in you.

Head:	*"I don't want to give up hope…"*
Inside Eyebrow:	*"Hope is all I have left."* (Sighs)
Outside Eyebrow:	*"Maybe someday she'll miss what we had…"*
Under Eye:	*"Maybe she will change her mind…"*
Nose:	*"And come back to me."*
Chin:	*"I know it's unlikely…"*
Collarbone:	*"Since it's been two years…"*
Under Arm:	*"But I still have hope."*

Head:	*"We were together for four years…"*
Inside Eyebrow:	*"Even though she never really committed to me…"*
Outside Eyebrow:	*"I was committed to her."*
Under Eye:	*"I thought it was only a matter of time."*
Nose:	*"I didn't want to believe I was wasting my time."* (Sighs)
Chin:	*"I couldn't stand to think it was all wasted…"*
Collarbone:	*"And that she was and is still stringing me along."*
Under Arm:	*"No, I couldn't stand that."*

Head:	*"But what if she is?"*
Inside Eyebrow:	*"What does that mean about me?"*
Outside Eyebrow:	*"It means I'm hopeless…"* (Laughs)
Under Eye:	*"Or hopeful…"*
Nose:	*"But I'm not dealing with reality."*
Chin:	*"A part of me knows this…"* (Sighs)
Collarbone:	*"But I don't want to admit it."*
Under Arm:	*"I'd rather pretend it's going to change…"*

Head:	*"Than go on with my life."*
Inside Eyebrow:	*"As long as I hang on to this hope…"*
Outside Eyebrow:	*"I don't have to face my aloneness."* (Sighs)
Under Eye:	*"Or deal with my part in these failed relationships."*
Nose:	*"I'd rather hang on to Pamela than know the truth."*

Chin:	*"I'd rather live in a fantasy…"*
Collarbone:	*"Than deal with reality."*
Under Arm:	*"Yes to fantasy. No to reality."*

Head:	*"Reality is too painful."*
Inside Eyebrow:	*"I don't think I'm up to it."*
Outside Eyebrow:	*"Instead I focus on Pamela and her needs."*
Under Eye:	*"I'd rather have the crumbs she throws me…"*
Nose:	*"Than the responsibility of a new relationship."*
Chin:	*"I feel too insecure about a new relationship…"*
Collarbone:	*"So I hang on to the old one."*
Under Arm:	*"I'm content with the crumbs."*

Head:	*"No, I'm not."*
Inside Eyebrow:	*"Yes, I am."* (Sighs)
Outside Eyebrow:	*"What if I want more than crumbs?"*
Under Eye:	*"There are all these other women who seem to like and accept me."*
Nose:	*"Why can't I be happy and move forward with one of them?"*
Chin:	*"I feel guilty – like I'm cheating on Pamela."*
Collarbone:	*"What if she finds out and dumps me?"* (Laughs)
Under Arm:	*"She's already dumped me…"*

Head:	*"I just want to pretend it never happened."*
Inside Eyebrow:	*"These other women are nice…"*
Outside Eyebrow:	*"But I hate starting over."*
Under Eye:	*"At least Pam knew my dark side…"*
Nose:	*"And accepted me for who I am…"*
Chin:	*"Or did she?"*
Collarbone:	*"Hey, wait! If she truly accepted me for who I am…"*
Under Arm:	*"Wouldn't we still be together?"* (Sighs)

We stop at this point to check in with Chuck and have him rate his current intensity level for the original statement:

"I don't want to give up the hope of Pamela's return."

It is now a seven. Therefore we create a modified tapping statement. Going back to tap on the karate chop point, Chuck repeats this aloud and with conviction:

"Even though I am still not ready to give up hope of Pam's returning, maybe there's someone better out there for me."

"Even though I am still not ready to give up hope of Pam's returning, maybe there's someone better out there for me."

"Even though I am still not ready to give up hope of Pam's returning, maybe there's someone better out there for me."

Then, going to the tapping points, follow along with each tapping phrase while tapping at least seven times on each point.

Head:	*"Maybe there's someone who will accept me for who I am…"*
Inside Eyebrow:	*"Maybe I need to accept myself first…"*
Outside Eyebrow:	*"Even though I don't feel worthy of acceptance."*
Under Eye:	*"But maybe someone else could help me learn to love and accept myself…"*
Nose:	*"Even though I don't right now."*
Chin:	*"I'd like to."*
Collarbone:	*"I'd like to love and accept myself."*
Under Arm:	*"But I don't know if I can…"*

Head:	*"I feel too damaged."*
Inside Eyebrow:	*"What if I start right now to love and accept myself..."* (Sighs)
Outside Eyebrow:	*"Despite feeling broken."*
Under Eye:	*"Let go of waiting for Pamela to love me back..."*
Nose:	*"And learn to love myself for a change."*
Chin:	*"Maybe that's more important..."*
Collarbone:	*"And maybe Pamela will want me back then."*
Under Arm:	*"See how hard it is for me to quit kidding myself."* (**Laughs**)

Head:	*"Or maybe I won't want her anymore."*
Inside Eyebrow:	*"Maybe I'll feel so good about myself..."*
Outside Eyebrow:	*"That her crumbs won't be enough for me anymore..."*
Under Eye:	*"That'd be great!"*
Nose:	*"No, that scares the crap out of me."*
Chin:	*"But I'm willing to entertain the possibility."*
Collarbone:	*"That I might not be willing to..."*
Under Arm:	*"Accept her crumbs anymore."*

Checking in with Chuck again, he now rates his intensity level for the original statement at a three. Since he knows how to continue tapping, let's assume he continues. For any of you reading along, by now I would hope that you, too, can continue to tap away any remaining intensity for your related issues.

Installation of Desired Beliefs

For Chuck, since this is such a difficult issue – one that has so many aspects, installing desired beliefs is critical. We selected these beliefs to reinforce and install:

"I am able to release people who don't really love me."

"I am worthy of love."

"I welcome women into my life who love and accept me, just as I now love and accept myself."

These are only a few of the affirming statements that Chuck (or you) might need. It's a good start. Tap several rounds on each of these statements to install them. Remember to tap in the same way as if you are removing a fear or self-limiting belief.

Outer Work: Set Me Free, Why Don't You Babe?

In this exercise you will create personalized tapping statements for yourself. Like a Chinese menu, combine one option from the first column with one from the second into a complete tapping statement using the following formula:

"Even though _____,
_____ *."*

Select one	Select an ending to the tapping statement
I am hanging on to someone from the past	I deeply love and release myself.
I'll always love _____	
I'm still secretly in love with _____	I deeply love and accept myself.
I hope that _____ will see the light and come back	

Select one	Select an ending to the tapping statement
I may never get over _____	What if I can?
I want _____ back	
My heart is broken because of _____	What if I do?
I can't stop thinking about _____	
I lost the love of my life	What if I just release it now?
I'll never forgive _____ for _____	
I'm still angry that _____ broke up with me	I deeply love and forgive myself.
I refuse to believe it's over with _____	
I'll never forgive myself for hurting _____	
I feel like I'm cheating on _____	
I wasted so much time on _____	
I am afraid to finally let go of _____	
It's been _____ since my divorce	
INSERT FAVORITE "FEAR" HEAR	

Here are examples:

> *"Even though* <u>I am afraid to finally let go of</u>   , <u>I deeply</u>
> <u>love and release myself.</u>

and

> *"Even though* <u>I'll always love</u>   , <u>What if I just</u>
> <u>release it now?</u>

Next rate the intensity level. Then start to tap as instructed in chapter 4. Feel free to adapt some of the tapping phrases from the examples throughout the book for your own use. Continue tapping until your intensity level reaches zero and, after testing, all additional aspects have been cleared.

What's Next?

In chapter 11 you will learn to use EFT to see yourself soul-matched. A SoulMate brings to the surface any unhealed aspects of yourself, so being soul-matched does not always feel good. This is why EFT is an essential tool for any ongoing SoulMate relationship.

Chapter 11
SEE YOURSELF SOUL-MATCHED:
MORE THAN THE SUM OF TWO HEARTS

"The question of how to be in a relationship is no other than the question of how to live."

JOHN WELWOOD

BEING SOUL-MATCHED means being with your spiritual and evolutionary partner and co-creating a relationship guided by Spirit. This hero's journey is not for the faint of heart; it is for the great of heart. SoulMates push each other's buttons and bring to the surface all that is unhealed in themselves. They do this not out of malice or intention, but in the course of opening more and more to love. SoulMates come together to burn off the dross of the ego and the illusions that keep their hearts small, closed off and limited. Loving someone deeply opens you up to the rawness of life.

Being soul-matched requires:

• **A beginner's mind**

• **An "I don't know it all" attitude**

- A willingness to embrace "both/and"

- A willingness to live on the razor's edge

- Letting go of the rules

- Letting your heart and soul lead the way

- Engaging in the deeper questions of life

This is no small order. You are seeking the place where you can hold both Heaven and Hell within and between you in order to distill the essence of life from them. In doing so, together you will experience both the rapture of being alive and the agony of ego death. It is the ultimate experience any human being can have. It is a transformation in service to the soul. It is the alchemy of love.

When accepting the call to embark upon this hero's journey, you leave the ordinary world behind. You can refuse the call, but at your own peril. In *The Hero with a Thousand Faces*, Joseph Campbell says, "One can only cling, like Satan, to oneself and be in hell; or else break, and be annihilated at last, in God." If you have yet to manifest your SoulMate, it is because you have not answered the call to adventure.

As you proceed on this journey, you will be greeted by the hounds of Hell. The hounds of Hell represent all your fears, doubts, internal demons and limitations. What faces you at this early juncture is the decision to move forward or remain and be torn apart. EFT banishes the hounds of Hell, allowing you to go deeper into the journey.

When you call out for assistance, the gods come, revealing resources you didn't know were available to you. These gifts come in the form of wise mentors (such as a SoulMate coach), synchronicities, epiphanies and God Winks™. They are moments of grace and guidance. Each gift demonstrates that you are indeed on your soul's path – the path of expanded consciousness, compassion, wisdom and the full utilization of your life in service to others.

SoulMate Synergy: More than the Sum of Two Hearts

To see yourself as soul-matched – as able to hold Heaven and Earth simultaneously in your relationship – is to envision, create, nurture and sustain the "we" between "me" and "s/he." In this way SoulMate relationships are synergistic. What you become together and give to the world is more than the sum of the talents, vision, and intentions each of you bring to the relationship. The "we" is greater than the "me." One definition of the word *synergism* is "The (Christian) doctrine that individual salvation is achieved through a combination of human will and divine grace." The "we" is where the Divine joins you in the creation of your SoulMate relationship.

Interestingly, most people have a greater capacity to imagine the darker aspects of a relationship than they do the brighter ones, perhaps because we're more familiar with or have come to expect Hell on Earth rather than Heaven. Television news and reality shows document stories of interminable fights that never get resolved, the high divorce rate and the extremes of suicides and murders in the name of love. We hear less about the heavenly, transformational aspects of love, other than the hype about sexual bliss that creates false expectations and standards none of us can consistently live up to. It's almost as if kindness, compassion and acts of service are not notable or newsworthy. Perhaps it is simply the fact that the ineffable, Heavenly realms of relationships are difficult to communicate. Where words fail, we know them by their actions.

Who would you need to be to stand in the fire of love's transformation? Who would you want standing beside you? What tools and resources would you want to take with you or discover on the journey? How do you envision the "we" handling both mundane reality and the more subtle aspects of Spirit?

> ## YOUR FAIRY GODMOTHER ASKS, *"Sacred or Scared?"*
>
> "Loving someone deeply is like a crucifixion. It is a joining of the higher with the lower – the spiritual and the material, where you transcend who you think you are and what you thought your life was about. It is not easy, nor is it meant to be easy. It is meant to awaken and transform you – particularly if you've chosen or been chosen by the SoulMate path.
>
> "It is the coming together of two forces – the yin and the yang of human experience, the interpenetration of the masculine and the feminine in the Divine cosmic dance of death and rebirth. On this battleground, love triumphs over ego. Be prepared for ego death. That's what it means, ultimately, to be soul-matched. Manifesting your SoulMate is a sacred path. Your ego will think you misspelled the word *scared.*"

Inner Work: Just My Imagination… Running Away with Me

As an attorney, Julie lives by logic and spends her days defending others who can't follow rules. Julie has been very successful doing this. Yet she longs for someone who shares her values of family and community service. Her life is busy with career, community service and things she does for herself. It is hard for her to imagine how she will fit one more thing into her overflowing life – even a SoulMate. It isn't logical; there will not be more hours in the day.

We discuss her lack of vision of an integrated life with her SoulMate. It is noteworthy that she chose to look for a man of depth by returning to church. Out of that conversation, we create the following tapping statement:

"Even though I have done all I know to do to find a man of depth, I choose to open myself to guidance from above."

This is very unlike Julie. She is driven, successful, intelligent and goal-oriented. She is accustomed to getting results through her own efforts – or so she assumes. Therefore the intensity level for this statement is a seven.

To begin, Julie repeats the following tapping statement aloud and with conviction three times while tapping on the karate chop point:

"Even though I have done all I know to do to find a man of depth, I choose to open myself to guidance from above."

"Even though I have done all I know to do to find a man of depth, I choose to open myself to guidance from above."

"Even though I have done all I know to do to find a man of depth, I choose to open myself to guidance from above."

Tap at least seven times on each point along with Julie as she repeats aloud the following tapping phrases:

Head:	*"I have done all I know to do."* (Sighs)
Inside Eyebrow:	*"That hasn't worked."*
Outside Eyebrow:	*"I am still single…"*
Under Eye:	*"And running out of time."* (Sighs)
Nose:	*"I am keeping my eyes open at church."*
Chin:	*"Hopeful that I will find a man of depth there…"*
Collarbone:	*"But so far, no luck."* (Sighs)
Under Arm:	*"Maybe I am doomed to be alone."*

Head:	*"I am so used to doing everything myself."*
Inside Eyebrow:	*"It's hard for me to ask for help…"*
Outside Eyebrow:	*"Or trust that help is available."*
Under Eye:	*"I am known for getting results."*
Nose:	*"Why is this so hard?"*
Chin:	*"I am so frustrated."* (Sighs)
Collarbone:	*"So frustrated."*
Under Arm:	*"This frustration…"*

Head:	*"I can't make this happen."*
Inside Eyebrow:	*"I am used to making things happen."* (Yawns)
Outside Eyebrow:	*"I am used to getting my way."* (Gasps)
Under Eye:	*"I guess God has other plans for me."*
Nose:	*"Like asking for his help."* (Yawns)
Chin:	*"What if I do ask for guidance?"*
Collarbone:	*"What if I get it?"*
Under Arm:	*"What if finding my SoulMate is not ONLY up to me?"*

Head:	*"I could use some help."*
Inside Eyebrow:	*"I'm just not used to needing help."*
Outside Eyebrow:	*"I can't imagine how that will work."*
Under Eye:	*"I don't see it working."*
Nose:	*"In fact, I don't envision my life being any different…"*
Chin:	*"Than it is now."*
Collarbone:	*"How am I going to make room for a SoulMate?"*
Under Arm:	*"Lord, help me!"* (Laughs)

Head:	*"If I can't even imagine it…"* (Sighs)
Inside Eyebrow:	*"How am I going to manifest it?"*
Outside Eyebrow:	*"I've been focusing on the wrong thing!"*
Under Eye:	*"I've been focused on the man, not the relationship."*

Nose:	*"The man, not the relationship."*
Chin:	*"Finding a warm somebody, not someone my soul desires."*
Collarbone:	*"Oops!"*
Under Arm:	*"Oops!"*

Head:	*"How do I get guidance from above?"*
Inside Eyebrow:	*"Would I recognize it?"*
Outside Eyebrow:	*"Would I listen?"*
Under Eye:	*"Probably not."*
Nose:	*"But what if I can?"*
Chin:	*"What if I tune in to my heart's desire..."* (Yawns)
Collarbone:	*"And my intuition..."*
Under Arm:	*"And be open to guidance."*

Head:	*"I can do that..."*
Inside Eyebrow:	*"But can I trust it?"*
Outside Eyebrow:	*"Will it work?"*
Under Eye:	*"So far nothing else has worked."*
Nose:	*"I have nothing to lose..."*
Chin:	*"And everything to gain."*
Collarbone:	*"Nothing to lose..."*
Under Arm:	*"And everything to gain."*

Head:	*"I am open to guidance from above."*
Inside Eyebrow:	*"And guidance from within."*
Outside Eyebrow:	*"Guidance from above..."*
Under Eye:	*"Guidance from within."*
Nose:	*"To help manifest my SoulMate."*
Chin:	*"There's more to life than I know..."*
Collarbone:	*"Or understand."*
Under Arm:	*"I'm just one person..."*

Head:	*"But I can call upon help…"*
Inside Eyebrow:	*"And guidance…"* (Yawns)
Outside Eyebrow:	*"I choose to trust and accept it."*
Under Eye:	*"I do want a SoulMate after all."*
Nose:	*"Why not accept help that comes from beyond myself?"*
Chin:	*"Since, apparently, I'm no good at this!"* (Laughs)
Collarbone:	*"Yes, I am."*
Under Arm:	*"No, I'm not."*

Because she's had a series of signals that her energy is shifting (sighs and yawns), we stop and check the intensity level of the original statement:

"Even though I have done all I know to do to find a man of depth, I choose to open myself to guidance from above."

It is now down to a three. What keeps it at a three is her unfamiliarity with the process of asking for and receiving guidance like this. A new tapping statement is developed to address this new aspect. Going back to tap on the karate chop point, she repeats the new tapping statement aloud and with conviction three times:

"Even though seeking guidance from above isn't familiar or comfortable, I choose to do it anyway."

"Even though seeking guidance from above isn't familiar or comfortable, I choose to do it anyway."

"Even though seeking guidance from above isn't familiar or comfortable, I choose to do it anyway."

Head:	*"This isn't familiar."*
Inside Eyebrow:	*"This isn't comfortable."*

Outside Eyebrow:	*"I'm not used to this."*
Under Eye:	*"But I'm open to it."*
Nose:	*"It might just work."*
Chin:	*"Either way, I'll be no worse off…"* (Sighs)
Collarbone:	*"For trying."*
Under Arm:	*"And it might work."*

Head:	*"A man of depth…"*
Inside Eyebrow:	*"Is probably tuned in to this, too."*
Outside Eyebrow:	*"So maybe by putting myself on this path…"*
Under Eye:	*"I will meet him…"*
Nose:	*"Because he's on the same path"*
Chin:	*"It'd be great to meet a man who…"*
Collarbone:	*"Is in touch with life's mystery…"* (Sighs)
Under Arm:	*"Not just some dry, logical overachiever that my dad wants for me."*

Head:	*"And who is just like me!"* (Gasps)
Inside Eyebrow:	*"No wonder I haven't met my SoulMate!"*
Outside Eyebrow:	*"I keep meeting men just like me."*
Under Eye:	*"All relationships are mirrors."*
Nose:	*"So maybe it's time I start…"*
Chin:	*"Living from the depths within myself…"*
Collarbone:	*"Instead of waiting for someone to come along…"*
Under Arm:	*"To show me how."*

Head:	*"Holy cow! No wonder I haven't met him yet."*
Inside Eyebrow:	*"I am not on his path… or mine."*
Outside Eyebrow:	*"I don't know if I can do this…"*
Under Eye:	*"But it is something I want."*
Nose:	*"It means a lot to me, though I've never understood why."*

Chin:	*"I've always said I wanted a man..."* (Sighs)
Collarbone:	*"Like this."*
Under Arm:	*"I didn't know I had to..."*

Head:	*"Live from my depths..."*
Inside Eyebrow:	*"Ask for guidance from above..."*
Outside Eyebrow:	*"To put myself in alignment with him."*
Under Eye:	*"Oh, silly me!"*
Nose:	*"I'm glad I see it now."*
Chin:	*"I don't know why..."*
Collarbone:	*"It never occurred to me before now."* (Yawns)
Under Arm:	*"I'm glad it occurred to me now."*

Head:	*"I can get comfortable with this."*
Inside Eyebrow:	*"In fact, I am kinda loving it!"*
Outside Eyebrow:	*"Kinda loving it."*
Under Eye:	*"I am so excited to learn how this will go."*
Nose:	*"Even though it's new and unfamiliar..."*
Chin:	*"I will become more and more comfortable."*
Collarbone:	*"More and more comfortable."* (Yawns)
Under Arm:	*"And so it is."*

At this point I have her stop and go back to rate the intensity level of the original statement. It is now a zero. Therefore it's time to test to see if she can find any other aspects that bring the intensity level back up. She reports that she is unable to do so.

Installation of Desired Beliefs

This is such an esoteric issue – seeking guidance from above and within. We selected these beliefs to reinforce and install:

"I easily recognize when I am being guided by Spirit."

"I quickly discern whether a man has the spiritual depth I seek."

"I trust that help is available."

These are only a few of the affirming statements that Julie (or you) might need. It's a good start. Tap several rounds on each of these statements to install them. Repeated tapping on these statements not only changes your beliefs, but it changes what manifests.

Outer Work: You May Say I'm a Dreamer

In this exercise you will create personalized tapping statements for yourself. Like a Chinese menu, combine one option from the first column with one from the second into a complete tapping statement using the following formula:

"Even though I don't see myself soul-matched because _____, _____."

Select one	Select an ending to the tapping statement
I haven't developed parts of myself	I deeply love and accept myself. (default)
I'm too busy to listen to my soul's direction	
I didn't think it could really happen	I choose to focus on this now.

Select one	Select an ending to the tapping statement
I'm afraid to claim this for myself	I stand in my full truth now.
I want to control everything	
It seems weird/impossible	I claim my birthright.
It's too much to hope for	
I doubt the Divine is interested in my life	I say yes to this now.
I can't imagine someone like this exists	
INSERT FAVORITE "HESITATION" HERE	

Here are examples:

> *"Even though I don't see myself soul-matched because* It seems weird/
> impossible, I say yes to this now.*"*

and

> *"Even though I don't see myself soul-matched because* I didn't think it could
> really happen, I choose to focus on this now.*"*

Next rate the intensity level. Then start to tap as instructed in chapter 4. Feel free to adapt some of the tapping phrases from the examples throughout the book for your own use. Continue tapping until your intensity level reaches zero and, after testing, all additional aspects have been cleared.

What's Next?

In chapter 12 you will learn the importance of surrender and letting Spirit guide you. This will drive your ego wild with fear. It will make you think you are crazy because your ego cannot fathom that there is something bigger than it is that is in control. Thankfully, removing fear is what EFT is best at.

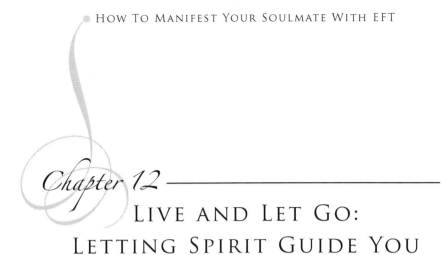

Chapter 12 —

LIVE AND LET GO:
LETTING SPIRIT GUIDE YOU

"Surrender is inner acceptance of what is without any reservations…surrender does not transform what is, at least not directly. It transforms you…"

ECKHART TOLLE

IN THE PROCESS of manifesting your SoulMate, surrender is the hardest part for most of us. We want to *do something* because we believe our own actions will get us the results we desire. When wanting or doing is locked in mortal battle against surrender, nothing *new* will manifest. *Surrender* is the radical acceptance of what is, with the certainty of more to come. The key to surrender is faith and patience – allowing the unknown to bring the unseen.

We sabotage this because we think we know better and need to be in control and active in pursuing a goal. All of this is just the ego being terrified of the unknown. To the ego, surrender feels like annihilation. That is because surrender is an act of soul, not an act of ego. It is wise to remember what is said in *A Course in Miracles* from the Foundation for Inner Peace: "Infinite patience produces immediate results."

Surrender is forming an alliance with the Divine to co-create reality. It is not giving up or becoming passive. It is partnering with the Divine to bring you the person your soul requires for its evolution and the fulfillment of your purpose. Instead of concealing your path, surrender reveals your path. It allows the fullest alignment and engagement of mind, body and spirit in manifesting your SoulMate. Surrender is living your life as a meditation or a prayer. The prayer is "Not my will, but Thine."

Surrender is the final stage. It's like in archery when, after aim and careful preparation, you release the arrow towards the target.

The Law of Attraction

Surrender activates the Law of Attraction. The Law of Attraction is a metaphysical process based on the assumptions that like attracts like and you get more of what you focus on. If you focus on lack, you get lack. If you focus on not having your SoulMate, you delay their manifestation. When you surrender and hold the spiritual belief of *unity* – that you are already deeply connected to your SoulMate – you speed their manifestation.

The Still, Small Voice Within

> *"Surrender is not just a religious concept: it's a powerful tool for listening to the voice of your spirit and following its directions."*
>
> SARA PADDISON

How do we know when the still, small voice is calling to us? I experience its call as a kind of restlessness and a sense of not being in the flow. I feel "off" and have a visceral sense that something is not right. I call it a "disturbance in the Force."

What is the still, small voice within? What does it sound like? Some say it is our conscience telling us right from wrong. Others say it is the voice of God speaking to us directly and personally. It's not some booming voice from above that sounds like Charlton Heston, Morgan Freeman or even George Burns; it is an internal communication that might not even come to you in the form of a voice, but more of a sensing or knowing – a gnosis. Mahatma Gandhi said, "If we have listening ears, God speaks to us in our own language, whatever that language be." Thank goodness! What would you do if your still, small voice spoke in ancient Babylonian?!

There are plenty of other voices in your head. Anyone who has practiced meditation can attest to that. Usually your mind is busy with your own thoughts, fears, plans, doubts, assumptions and internal criticisms. Therefore, as you cultivate the ability to listen for the still, small voice within, discernment is essential.

In my discernment process, the questions I ask about each message I receive are:

- **Is it compassionate?**

- **Is it caring?**

- **Is it kind?**

- **Is this action in the best interest and highest good of all involved?**

If you have that, you're in the presence of Spirit, and you can trust. After you hear it and follow its guidance, you have surrendered to the Divine – the transcendent. Transcendent of what? The ego.

Take Inspired Action

"Love and do what you will."

ST. AUGUSTINE

Inspired action comes from the guidance of Spirit, not ego. When in doubt, don't. Inspired action is responsive, not reactive. When gripped by fear, tap or "take the one seat." Buddhist teacher Jack Kornfield says, "When we take the one seat on our meditation cushion we become our own monastery. We create the compassionate space that allows for the arising of all things: sorrows, loneliness, shame, desire, regret, frustration, happiness."

Before you act, find your center. Ground yourself in Spirit. Set ego aside. Ask yourself, "How do I want to *be* about this? What would love do?" Then do that. With good intention and inspired action, good results follow. It's karma.

Your Fairy Godmother Says, "Peak-a-Boo!"

"Surrender doesn't have to be a heavy, solemn thing. It can be a joyous relief. Finally the burden is off you.

"Surrender can be playful – like a game of Peak-a-Boo with the Divine. 'Now you see me; now you don't. Peak-a-boo! Here I am!' This is how children learn that you are there even though they can't see you.

"We're all playing Peak-a-Boo with the Divine. Surrender helps you see it in unexpected ways, places and times. Surprise! Here I am!

"When you surrender, you live in eager anticipation of the surprise. The dual weights of yearning and despair are cast off. Surrender creates equanimity and bliss because you release yourself from any attachment to the results."

Inner Work: Surrender, Surrender...
But Don't Give Yourself Away

Julie is in a time crunch to have a baby within the next three years. She admits to having difficulties with this idea of surrender. She thinks it will take too long.

"I struggle to surrender and allow Spirit to bring my SoulMate to me."

For this session, we are going to start with the tapping statement:

"Even though I struggle to surrender to Spirit because I am afraid that it will take too long, I deeply love and accept myself."

She always starts by determining her intensity level. In this case it was an eight. She begins, as always, by tapping on the karate chop point while repeating the entire tapping statement three times aloud and with conviction:

"Even though I struggle to surrender to Spirit because I am afraid that it will take too long, I deeply love and accept myself."

"Even though I struggle to surrender to Spirit because I am afraid that it will take too long, I deeply love and accept myself."

"Even though I struggle to surrender to Spirit because I am afraid that it will take too long, I deeply love and accept myself."

Follow along so as to borrow the benefits as Julie taps at least seven times on each of the following tapping points:

Head:	*"I'm afraid to surrender."*
Inside Eyebrow:	*"I'm afraid to surrender."* (Sigh)

Outside Eyebrow: *"I've accomplished everything on my own so far."*

Under Eye: *"Or have I?"*

Nose: *"I am in a hurry."*

Chin: *"I am afraid this will take too long."*

Collarbone: *"I am in a hurry."*

Under Arm: *"I am afraid this will take too long.*

Head: *"I've waited too long!"*

Inside Eyebrow: *"What if it's too late already?"*

Outside Eyebrow: *"What if it's too late already?"*

Under Eye: *"And I've just waited too long."*

Nose: *"I'll never have what I want."*

Chin: *"Unless this works!"* (Sigh)

Collarbone: *"What have I got to lose?"*

Under Arm: *"I guess I could give this a try."*

Head: *"I am willing to give this a try…"*

Inside Eyebrow: *"Because I haven't been successful on my own with this."*

Outside Eyebrow: *"I haven't been successful on my on with this."*

Under Eye: *"I thought once I decided I was ready…"*

Nose: *"It would just happen."*

Chin: *"I thought once I decided I was ready…"*

Collarbone: *"It would just happen."*

Under Arm: *"I guess not!"*

Head: *"I really want to have a family."*

Inside Eyebrow: *"But I don't think that's ever going to happen."* (Sniffles)

Outside Eyebrow: *"I really wanted a family…"*

Under Eye: *"To replace my broken one."* (Gasps!)

Nose: *"My poor broken family."*

Chin:	*"I feel so sorry for Dad."*
Collarbone:	*"I want to make him happy."*
Under Arm:	*"Give him grandchildren."*
Head:	*"Give him a happy life."*
Inside Eyebrow:	*"Give him what he wants."*
Outside Eyebrow:	*"Hey! What about what I want?"*
Under Eye:	*"What about what I want?"*
Nose:	*"What about giving me what I want?"*
Chin:	*"What do I really want?"*
Collarbone:	*"I really want less responsibility."*
Under Arm:	*"I want a home and family…"*
Head:	*"And less responsibility."*
Inside Eyebrow:	*"Maybe I don't have to want what Dad wants for me."*
Outside Eyebrow:	*"Maybe it's okay for me to have just what I want for me."*
Under Eye:	*"Maybe I can surrender to my own wants and desires…"*
Nose:	*"And let Dad do the same for himself."*
Chin:	*"He seems happy now…"*
Collarbone:	*"But I don't want to upset him."*
Under Arm:	*"I've always been his little girl."*
Head:	*"Hey! I'm not a little girl anymore."*
Inside Eyebrow:	*"I am a grown woman."*
Outside Eyebrow:	*"Not a little girl anymore…"*
Under Eye:	*"I am a grown woman."*
Nose:	*"Maybe it's time for me to decide what I want…"*
Chin:	*"And go for it."*
Collarbone:	*"Maybe it's time for me to decide what I want…"*
Under Arm:	*"And go for it."* (Yawns)

Head:	*"Dad just wants me to be happy."*
Inside Eyebrow:	*"He's taken care of."*
Outside Eyebrow:	*"It's my time to be happy."*
Under Eye:	*"It's my time to be happy."*
Nose:	*"I surrender to my happiness."*
Chin:	*"I surrender to manifesting my dreams…"*
Collarbone:	*"Even if I'm not quite sure what they are."*
Under Arm:	*"Even if I'm not quite sure how that is going to happen."*

It is time to check in with Julie. Her intensity level started at an eight. She's now down to a four and smiling a bit. We decide to continue with this modified tapping statement, which she repeats aloud and with conviction three times while tapping on the karate chop point:

"Even though I STILL struggle to surrender to Spirit because I am afraid that it will take too long, I deeply love and accept myself."

"Even though I STILL struggle to surrender to Spirit because I am afraid that it will take too long, I deeply love and accept myself."

"Even though I STILL struggle to surrender to Spirit because I am afraid that it will take too long, I deeply love and accept myself."

Now we go back to tapping on the tapping points while saying the following tapping phrases aloud and with conviction:

Head:	*"I'm still struggling to surrender to Spirit."*
Inside Eyebrow:	*"I don't even know what that means."*
Outside Eyebrow:	*"After surrendering to Dad's wants for me all these years…"*
Under Eye:	*"I'm not sure I'm ready to surrender anything to*

anyone right now!" (Gasps!)

Nose:	*"I don't want to surrender to Spirit or anyone!"*
Chin:	*"No more surrendering..."*
Collarbone:	*"No wonder it's so hard for me to surrender!"*
Under Arm:	*"I've been doing it all my life."*

Head:	*"Surrendering my wants to others all my life."*
Inside Eyebrow:	*"Surrendering my wants to others all my life"* (Sighs)
Outside Eyebrow:	*"Holy cow!"*
Under Eye:	*"No wonder I haven't manifested a SoulMate."*
Nose:	*"I was busy trying to find someone for Dad!"*
Chin:	*"Busy trying to find someone Dad liked..."*
Collarbone:	*"Instead of someone I liked."* (Yawns)
Under Arm:	*"Time for me to surrender to what I want."*

Head:	*"I knew this, but I didn't really know this..."*
Inside Eyebrow:	*"Until now."*
Outside Eyebrow:	*"It's about time I rebelled, don't you think?"*
Under Eye:	*"It's about time..."*
Nose:	*"About time..."*
Chin:	*"About time I did what I wanted for me."*
Collarbone:	*"And I want this to work."*
Under Arm:	*"I choose to surrender to Spirit this time."*

Head:	*"Not because I have to..."*
Inside Eyebrow:	*"But because I choose to!"*
Outside Eyebrow:	*"No wonder the idea of surrender was so hard for me."*
Under Eye:	*"I've been doing it all my life!"*
Nose:	*"Surrendering to what others want for me..."*
Chin:	*"Not what I want for myself."*
Collarbone:	*"Time for that to change!"* (Laughs)
Under Arm:	*"I'm overdue for a change on that."*

Head:	*"Way overdue…"*
Inside Eyebrow:	*"No wonder this was hard."*
Outside Eyebrow:	*"From now on I choose whom to surrender to."*
Under Eye:	*"I say who…"*
Nose:	*"I say when…"*
Chin:	*"I say where…"*
Collarbone:	*"It's up to me now…"*
Under Arm:	*"Me and Spirit."*

Head:	*"That's a better choice…"*
Inside Eyebrow:	*"Because I know Spirit will do right by me."*
Outside Eyebrow:	*"Spirit will do right by me."* (Yawn)
Under Eye:	*"Even though I used to have problems with this idea of surrender…"*
Nose:	*"I see why now…"*
Chin:	*"And I make a conscious choice to trust Spirit…"*
Collarbone:	*"Trust Spirit to do right by me…"*
Under Arm:	*"And help manifest MY SoulMate… not Dad's choice."*

It's time to check in and see how intense the original tapping statement feels for Julie right now:

"I struggle to surrender to Spirit because I am afraid that it will take too long."

The intensity level now is at zero. She comments, "It doesn't bother me now. I am choosing to surrender to Spirit instead of Dad. I trust Spirit to do right by me."

Now that her intensity is at a zero, it's time to have her test to see if she can make the intensity level go back up. She closes her eyes and repeats the original tapping statement silently to herself to notice what happens. When she opens her eyes, she says, "I'm no longer afraid to surrender to

Spirit, but I am still worried that it will take too long."

Because we've worked together using EFT on many other aspects during the process of manifesting her SoulMate, Julie knows how to create her own tapping statement for that new aspect and work on that by herself.

Installation of Desired Beliefs

Surrender is an esoteric, counter-intuitive issue and spiritual principle. We selected these beliefs to reinforce and install:

"I surrender the timing of meeting my SoulMate."

"I surrender in order to manifest my dreams."

"I trust Spirit to do right by me."

These are only a few of the affirming statements that Julie (or you) might need. It's a good start. Tap several rounds on each of these statements to install them. Tap on these until you no longer question their veracity and validity in your life.

Outer Work: My Endless Love

In this exercise you will create personalized tapping statements for yourself. Like a Chinese menu, combine one option from the first column with one from the second into a complete tapping statement using the following formula:

"Even though I struggle to surrender to Spirit because _____, _____."

Select one	Select an ending for the tapping statement
I think I have to take control	I deeply love and accept myself.
I don't trust this will work	
I'm afraid what will happen	What if this works?
I don't believe in doing so	
My ego thinks it's in charge	What if I let it be easy?
I've never tried it before	
I don't understand how this works	I choose to do so anyway.
I want to keep doing this my way	
I think I know better	I release my fear of doing so.
It's hard	
I don't know how	I allow this.
It will take too long	
INSERT FAVORITE "RATIONALIZATION" HERE	

Here are examples:

"Even though I struggle to surrender because <u>I think I know better, I choose to do so anyway.</u>"

and

"Even though I struggle to surrender because <u>It's hard</u>, <u>What if this works?</u>"

Next rate the intensity level. Then start to tap as instructed in chapter 4. Feel free to adapt some of the tapping phrases from the examples throughout the book for your own use. Continue tapping until your intensity level reaches zero and, after testing, all additional aspects have been cleared.

What's Next?

Chapter 13 provides suggestions for things to do when you think EFT is not working. There are some additional steps and procedures to augment the basic EFT technique that you've learned and practiced so far.

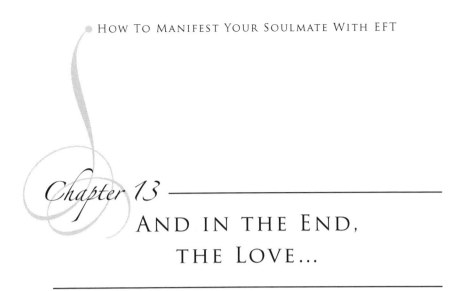

Chapter 13 —————————————
AND IN THE END,
THE LOVE...

—————————————————————————

Signs that Your Inner Work *is* Working

ASIDE FROM ACTUALLY manifesting your SoulMate, synchronicities, equanimity and gratitude are the three main signs that your inner work is working and you are on the right path to manifesting your SoulMate.

Synchronicity – When the Transcendent Rubber Meets the Road to Love

> *"Synchronicity is a mind-boggling and sometimes eerie*
> *rendezvous between the world and our inner selves."*

> ☞ DAVID RICHO

Forty years ago I first heard this startling statement: "When the student is ready, the teacher will come." That was my first introduction to the concepts of synchronicity and manifestation. It took my breath away. Was there some force working in the world, perhaps even in my own life, that was here to assist me in fulfilling my destiny? Note the emphasis for the student is on *readiness* that leads to the *inevitability* of the teacher's arrival. The same is true for your SoulMate. When you, the lover, are ready, your SoulMate will inevitably come. The two currents of your life mission and purpose and their life mission and purpose are on a collision course. It is only a matter of time.

When two currents collide, eddies are created. According to the National Ocean Service, "The swirling motion of eddies in the ocean cause nutrients that are normally found in colder, deeper waters to come to the surface." What a great metaphor for the comingling of SoulMates! Together you will bring something from the unconscious to the surface that nurtures or serves all of life. The sum of your two lives creates a synergism.

Swiss psychiatrist Carl Jung described *synchronicity* as an "acausal connecting principle" or "meaningful coincidence." Jung based this principle on his study of quantum physics. Others refer to synchronistic moments as "grace" or "divine providence." I tend to view synchronicities as proof that I am on the right path. It's like a pat on the back from God.

The moment you meet your SoulMate is the ultimate synchronicity. Lucky is the person who recognizes in that very moment the intersection of the perfect time, perfect place and perfect person. When people talk about being in sync with each other, what they recognize is an alignment of wants, mission, values and, dare I say, chakras – the body's energy centers. SoulMates resonate on many levels. Something deep in me recognizes something deep in you that is sacred.

Equanimity

Abraham Maslow revised his emphasis on *peak experiences* in his book, *Religion, Values and Peak-Experiences*. He added a "greater consideration" for what he called *plateau experiences*. Plateau experiences are more voluntary and long-lasting than peak experiences. Also they are more serene, quietly blissful and contemplative than the more emotionally dramatic peak experiences. A peak experience is a transient episode that seems to happen in a serendipitous manner, but which passes quickly. Infatuation with a new love prospect is a peak experience. You are excited. The world feels whole and everything looks clearer and more beautiful and smells sweeter. You feel vibrantly alive, connected to everything and everybody, but especially to your new love.

Equanimity is a plateau experience – a state of being entered into by choice and taking the one seat. The entire process of manifesting your SoulMate described in this book is a way to enter this state of being. You feel like you have come home to the essence of yourself, which is love.

A plateau experience is the ongoing equanimity and connection you feel when you recognize that you *are* your own SoulMate. You feel at home and peaceful within yourself, no matter what is going on in your love life.

When you have manifested your SoulMate in physical space and time, this equanimity continues no matter what is going on between you. Even if your egos are at odds, you recognize and remember that you are connected at a deep level – at the soul level. You are together for the purpose of releasing ego and healing hurts that block you from this profound level of connection. Remembering this gives you the calm and confidence to sort through what has arisen between you. A dear friend of mine once said to me when we were at odds, "I'm mad at you and want you to go away. However, YOU are the one person I most want to talk to about this!" In doing so he validated our deeper connection that superseded the transient issue between us.

Gratitude

> "*The secret to manifesting anything that you desire is your willingness and ability to realign yourself so that your inner world is in harmony with the power of intention.*"

WAYNE DYER

Here is an experience that exemplifies the kind of gratitude and equanimity I am talking about: Once upon a time I was caught up in the middle of my own suffering, thinking I had just blown it with a potential SoulMate.

I went to Trader Joe's for my usual supplies. When the clerk asked me how I was doing, I responded, "FABULOUS!"

"Are you always fabulous or did something fabulous just happen?" he asked.

"I'm always fabulous, but it took me a long time to get there."

A middle-aged woman standing behind me in line asked, "Do you have a recipe for that?"

"Yes… gratitude."

The way to align with what you desire to manifest is gratitude – both for what is and what will come to you. Gratitude is both a cause and effect of the manifesting process. It might seem odd to be grateful for the impediments in your life. As you learned from the story of Fatima in chapter 3, impediments are essential to your SoulMate path. As her story demonstrated, they are the vehicles to your destiny. You are always, always being guided to fulfill your purpose, even when it is not clear to you or not on your time schedule.

Now my response to conflict or "bad" things happening is, "Good or bad… who can say?" Be grateful all the time… for everything. It's all God!

Inner Work: I Don't Want to Spoil the Party

One of the things that stops people from using EFT is not knowing what to say while tapping. Or they think it's not working because 1) the results come with little or no effort, 2) they aren't able to personalize it for their particular situation or 3) they haven't mastered working with aspects. That's how the idea for this book came to me. EFT is such a powerful tool that I want to remove these barriers. By helping you personalize and apply this tool within the manifestation process, you can and will manifest your SoulMate. It is inevitable if you do all the steps contained in this book.

To be successful using EFT, make sure you follow these guidelines recommended by Gary Craig and other EFT masters:

1. **Choose an issue that has intensity in the present moment.** If there is no intensity, there is nothing to work on. It's that simple. State your issue as a fear, if possible.

2. **Be specific.** EFT works best when you create tapping statements that are specific to your issues, memories, upset or physical pain. Describe *exactly* what the upset is, how it feels in your body and what situation it is connected to. For example, instead of saying, *"Even though I'm anxious..."* you might try, *"Even though I feel tension in my shoulders and neck, my heart is racing and I'm sweating when I think about asking Alice out on a date, I deeply love and accept myself."* If the issue is a painful past memory, give as much detail as needed to make it come alive in your mind. For example, *"Even though I believed my mother when she said, 'You're too selfish for anybody to love you,' I deeply love and accept myself."* If you are still attached to your ex, you could create the following tapping statement: *"Even though I still think about Tom every morning when I wake up, wondering if he'll ever call me, I deeply love and accept myself."*

3. **Say it like you mean it.** When repeating your tapping statement aloud, make sure to say it like you mean it. Say it with conviction. If you just repeat it in a rote fashion, with a flat voice, it won't feel like it has any intensity.

4. **Add humor.** Doctors Steve Wells and David Lake taught me this. If you can laugh at yourself, your energy will shift. Try exaggerating what you are saying while you tap. If you are upset, try whining. If you are angry, try growling.

5. **Be persistent.** Keep tapping. Watch for the spontaneous sighs or yawns that indicate your energy is shifting and internal blockages are being released. One of the biggest mistakes is quitting too soon. Tap until the intensity level falls to zero. Don't just accept a little improvement. In the tapping sequences in this book, I only had space for a few rounds of tapping. I have been known to tap for up to 45 minutes with a client on a difficult or complex issue.

    People ask me how often they should tap. If you are serious about manifesting your SoulMate, tap every day. Set aside some time each day that is sacred to do this work. You won't be sorry.

6. **Tap away your doubts.** Perhaps you don't believe it will work for you, so you don't keep at it. If so, you might tap on *"Even though I don't believe EFT is going to work for me, what if it does?"*

7. **Tap while looking in the mirror.** I discovered this myself and find it to be extremely helpful. Rarely do I tap without looking in a mirror. It seems to magnify the intensity of the work. Often I need a box of tissue nearby! I can watch the expressions on my face change from sadness or distress to joy as I clear issues. That is reinforcing.

8. **Use the tender spot.** Instead of tapping on the karate chop point to start, try rubbing the tender spot (sometimes called the sore spot) while saying your tapping statement aloud three times, as before. The tender spot is located just inside of your shoulder, under your collarbone. Then go on to use the rest of the tapping points as usual. This change might be just what you need.

9. **Tap on the new aspects as they arise.** Again, this requires persistence. Often issues are complex and have multiple aspects. An aspect can be another belief, fear or memory associated with the same issue. Often an issue persists because you haven't cleared all relevant aspects yet. Not

all issues can be cleared by tapping on a single aspect. In fact, most issues have multiple aspects. Sometimes the way aspects are connected is like a daisy chain; when one gets cleared another presents itself.

10. **Remember to test.** Testing in EFT comes after you have reduced the intensity of the issue you're working on to zero. There are several ways to test whether EFT worked. The most obvious is to see if you behave or feel differently in the actual situation. If you cleared the fears of asking Alice out, then give her a call. If any emotional intensity arises anywhere in the process, there are other aspects to clear around this issue. A second way to test to see if an issue is cleared is by using your imagination. State your original issue aloud. Close your eyes. Using your imagination, see if you can increase the intensity of the distress you feel about that issue. What, if anything, do you need to see, think, remember or feel to make the intensity level go back up? I often hear clients say "I'm not getting anything" when the issue is cleared. If there other aspects connected to the original issue, this is where they might show up and cause the intensity level to spike again. Treat each aspect as a new issue. Create a new tapping statement and repeat the entire tapping sequence for that aspect.

11. **Add the 9 gamut procedure.** The *9 gamut procedure* is an addition to the basic EFT recipe that allows your brain to access and process information apart from the effects of tapping on the body's acupuncture points. I add it when the intensity level isn't dropping no matter how long I tap. You perform the 9 gamut procedure by first locating the *gamut point* on the back of your hand. It is a half inch behind the midpoint between the knuckle of the ring finger and the knuckle of the little finger. While continuously tapping this point, perform the following nine different actions in this order:

1. Close your eyes for a second or two.
2. Open your eyes.

3. Eyes down hard right, while holding your head steady.

4. Eyes down hard left, while holding your head steady.

5. Roll your eyes in a clockwise circle.

6. Roll your eyes in a counter-clockwise circle.

7. Hum two seconds of a song, like "Happy Birthday."*

8. Count rapidly from one to five.

9. Hum two seconds of the song again.

Most people use "Happy Birthday" as their tune unless some bad feelings or trauma are associated with that song or their birthday. In that case, any tune you associate with happy feelings will do. You might choose "You Are My Sunshine" instead.

12. **Get a drink of water.** Sometimes tapping doesn't work optimally when you are dehydrated. Your energetic system can be thought of like a car battery. It used to be that you occasionally had to put water in a car battery to help it hold a charge. If you are dehydrated, it's like having a low battery. Drink some water and try again.

13. **Wait until later.** Sometimes things we cannot detect interfere with the ability of tapping to work. I know that sounds like an excuse, but certain medications and/or foods can interfere. Waiting will allow your body to metabolize them. Try again later.

14. **Tap in anticipation of distress.** Have you ever been dumped via email? I have. If I think an email contains something potentially upsetting, I tap before, during and after reading it. Not only does this prevent distress, but it makes me willing and more able to face unpleasantness.

15. **Don't stop.** Some of my clients are reluctant to use EFT because they are concerned that by focusing on the negative they are creating or reinforcing it. You don't need to be afraid to tap while saying something negative such as *"Even though I feel terrified when…"*. The truth

is you're not making it worse. The issue is already there. You're just shining a light on it for the purpose of clearing it. If you are tempted to give up because of this fear, tap on *"Even though I don't want to tap because I'm afraid of making it worse, what if it helps?"*

Outer Work: I've Been Waiting for a Girl [Guy] Like You...

> *"Waiting does not exist in the experience of those who recognize the presence of love wherever they are."*
>
> ALAN COHEN

Once you truly surrender, you won't feel like you are waiting anymore. You won't know how quickly or where your SoulMate will show up. Prepare to be surprised! However, if you need something to do in the meantime, here are a few suggestions:

- If you have skipped any steps in the stages of manifesting, go back and redo them.

- Continue writing to your SoulMate in present time to further develop that relationship.

- Bask daily in the feeling/certainty of having your SoulMate in your life.

- Continue to live an authentic, full, happy, purposeful life.

- Live with positive expectations that what you want is what you will receive.

- Love and nurture yourself.

- Pay attention to the still, small voice.

- Keep track of what your intuition is saying.

- Take inspired action.

- Go outside of your comfort zone.

- Take note of synchronicities and God Winks™.

- Address fears and impatience with EFT, should they arise.

- Stay clear of emotional vultures and negative, skeptical people.

- Create a vision board or collage that represents your SoulMate story.

- Feng shui your home to enhance the flow of energy into your relationship corner.

- Clear out space in your calendar so there is time to spend with your SoulMate.

- Clear out a drawer, a shelf in the medicine cabinet and a section of your closet if you wish your SoulMate to come live with you.

- Dance!

- Do all the things now that you were waiting to do until *after* your SoulMate arrived!

YOUR FAIRY GODMOTHER SAYS,
"One More Thing..."

"Whew! This is a lot to digest and transform into SoulMate gold. You might feel like you'll be tapping forever. (You could tap about that! *"Even though I'm afraid I'll be tapping forever, I deeply love and accept myself."*) The good news is that you don't have to remove absolutely every single barrier that stands between you and your SoulMate. You just have to remove enough of them.

"No, you don't have to be perfect or completely healed and whole to manifest your SoulMate, and neither do they. Otherwise what soul-work would you have to do together? You manifested each other to learn vital soul lessons, to grow personally and develop spiritually, to fulfill a higher purpose and to become a channel for Divine love into the world.

"Yes, there will be rough times with your SoulMate, especially when you run up against your remaining ego barriers or trigger them in each other. It is how you handle that challenge that characterizes a SoulMate relationship. When you both make the radical commitment to mutual unfolding and being open to the rawness and beauty of life itself, then you know you have met your SoulMate.

"It is hard to say good-bye. This has been a beautiful journey that we've taken together. Welcome to the kinship of SoulMates and master manifestors.

"You and your SoulMate are pioneers on the frontier of spiritual partnerships. You are the cusp of the next evolutionary wave. As architects of true SoulMate relationships, you are the Magellans of inner space. Let the abundant joy of Spirit flow through you out into the world.

"I celebrate you and bow to the Divinity within your unity.

"Namasté!"

ACKNOWLEDGEMENTS

SINCE I WAS quite young something in me always oriented towards spirituality and questions about the "farthest reaches of human nature." I didn't choose it. It chose me. I want to thank my dad, who even as a devout Catholic demonstrated a lively curiosity about paranormal experiences, past lives and psychic abilities. His example allowed me to explore and develop my imagination, thus keeping the portal open to the Divine. That helped. When I was eight and had the intuition that we were all innately divine, I paid attention.

It is only proper to acknowledge that this book is part of a long path that I have felt compelled to follow – a path of never-ending mystery and adventure that leaves me both quivering with awe and quaking with fear. This book is a manifestation of my relationship with what I choose to call the Holy Spirit, who is my ultimate SoulMate.

I wish to thank the Holy Spirit for bringing just the right situations, people and experiences into my life to make this book possible. For inspiring me to recognize writing as a transformational tool, I wish to thank my college English teachers, Michael DeCarbo and Charles "Skip" Radey. For guiding me through the process of developing this book, I wish to thank my book coach, publisher and kindred spirit, Lynne Klippel.

Of course, I wish to thank all my EFT teachers for developing and disseminating this transformational tool to the world: Gary Craig, Steve Wells, David Lake and Carol Solomon.

Although I have not met any of these men personally, I have learned so much from their writings. Therefore, I wish to thank C. G. Jung, David Spangler, Joseph Campbell, David Richo and John Welwood for being the pioneers and visionaries who shaped my thinking and influenced the perspective I put forth in this book.

Finally, I wish to thank my clients, students and friends who inspired me by their willingness to struggle and grow. _∽_

About Annette Vaillancourt, Ph.D.
The Elite SoulMate Coach

Annette Vaillancourt, Ph.D., has one enviable superpower: She is a master manifestor. Her passion is pushing the envelope of consciousness beyond the limits of ego. To do so, she is committed to "practical mysticism" – attending to and enacting the messages from Spirit in everyday life.

A social introvert and recovering shy person, Annette has accomplished every goal she set for herself. It makes sense then, that she would share her love of manifesting to help others accomplish similar goals using the secrets she has learned.

After 24+ years as a couple's counselor, she turned her attention from trying to resurrect broken marriages to helping spiritually minded singles manifest their SoulMates. Her work is inspired by the poet Rumi's line: *"Your task is not to seek for love, but merely to seek and find all the barriers within yourself that you have built against it."* She blames Kenny Loggins for sparking her interest in transformative love and conscious relationship as a spiritual path.

Her clients are spiritual singles and cultural creatives who are drawn to personal growth and spiritual practices and want to use their relationships to evolve, serve, and manifest more love in the world.

Annette holds a Ph.D. in counseling psychology from Southern Illinois University, an M.A. in counseling psychology from Ball State University and a B.S. in psychology from Central Michigan University. She has presented at over 300 workshops to groups ranging from local school teachers to Fortune 500 companies. She wrote a monthly newspaper column for five years, hosted a bi-monthly Blog Talk Radio show, and organized St. Louis Spiritual Singles, St. Louis Holistic Share and Saint Louis EFT – Emotional Freedom Technique MeetUp groups.

Annette currently lives and loves abundantly in the St. Louis metro area. She enjoys playing the fiddle/violin, dancing, occasional modeling and has earned a Brown Belt in Shotokan karate.

For more information about the author or to sign up for her free mailing list, visit: www.ManifestYourSoulMateWithEFT.com